ELBERT V. BOWDEN
State University of New York
College at Fredonia

Economics Through The Looking Glass

D1222632

Canfield Press ℶ San Francisco
A Department of Harper & Row, Publishers, Inc.
New York   Evanston   London

ECONOMICS THROUGH THE LOOKING GLASS

Copyright © 1974 by Elbert V. Bowden

74   75   76   10 9 8 7 6 5 4 3 2 1

Library of Congress Cataloging in Publication Data

Bowden, Elbert V
    Economics through the looking glass

    1. Economics—History.   2. Economic History
I. Title.
HB75.B7766   330'.09   74-11179
ISBN 0-06-380850-1

PREFACE

Remember the joke about frogs? One Friday afternoon the little boy asked the librarian to help him find a book about frogs. Together they selected a big book that explained almost *everything* about frogs. The following Monday the boy returned the book. The surprised librarian said, "You have read through this big book *already*?"

"No, I didn't. But I want to return it, anyway."

"You didn't *like* the book?"

"No, it wasn't that. It was just that this book was trying to tell me *more* about frogs than I *wanted to know* about frogs."

The moral of the story: When a book tries to tell you more than you want to know about something, likely the book will wind up not telling you anything.

Aren't "we professors," every day, turning students off to history, denying them historical perspective on current conditions and issues and problems—just because we are trying to tell students more about frogs than they want (or need) to know (or will ever remember) about frogs? I think so. This I promise: In this little book I will try very hard not to do that.

Some books should indeed give detailed descriptions and explanations of historical conditions and events. But we need some books of the other kind, too: books which show the overview, the forest instead of the trees; books which show the broad, rapid sweep of historical change, and show the present for what it is—a fleeting moment in the *continuing flow* of history.

This book has but one purpose: to place the economic realities of today—the conditions, problems, and ideas—in historical perspective, to provide an awareness of where we are today compared to yesterday, and thereby provide for better insight into today, and tomorrow.

There isn't much historical detail in this book. The flow of thought moves rapidly from one period to another, from one developer of ideas to another, touching the highlights, gathering the threads and trying to pull them all together.

The writing style in this book reflects my personal convictions:

> that the easier the reading, the more it will be read and the better it will be understood, for the task at hand is tough enough without compounding it by couching the explanations in language unfamiliar to the student;

> that scholarly prose is not an efficient medium for the transmission of deep, basic thoughts to students, for there's no idea so deep, no theory so rigorous that it can't be explained in simple English (if one knows his ideas, and his English—and is willing to put in the time required to do it);

> that one of the reasons students don't see the *flow* of history is that they spend so much time stumbling over scholarly vocabulary and syntax; in short, that learning can be (and whenever possible *should* be) fun.

The *facts* of history, once learned, are easily forgotten. But an awareness of the *flow* of history, once gained, is never lost. Everyone can gain this awareness—can learn to see himself and his world, and his academic subject (here economics) as a part of this evolutionary sweep—from yesterday, to today, to tomorrow. I have tried to design this little book to help you the reader to gain this awareness in economics. And I hope I don't tell you any more than you want to know about frogs—or anything else. I would like to acknowledge the significant debt which this book owes to Robert Heilbroner. My ideas about how to conceptualize and synthesize the history of economics and the economic history of the world have been greatly influenced by his *The Worldly Philosophers* and *The Making of Economic Society*. Had he not made those great leaps forward I would not have been able to make this small one. Also, I make an acknowledgment to Alvin Toffler, author of *Future Shock,* whose influence on my thinking about the speed and impact of change is evident at various places throughout the book.

My sincerest appreciation to Professors Maryanna Boynton, Ann N. P. Fisher, Warren L. Fisher, Kanji Haitani, Richard K. Hay and Kenneth M. Parzych, whose careful criticisms and suggestions on earlier drafts have resulted in many improvements; and to Mary Ann Burgess, without whose secretarial skills and cooperative attitude in the face of ridiculous demands this book would never have made it.

Elbert V. Bowden
Fredonia, New York

CONTENTS

INTRODUCTION

For more than ten thousand centuries people have been roaming around on various parts of the earth. That's right— more than *ten thousand centuries!* All this time these people have been struggling to make it, trying to choose the best ways of using their limited resources to meet their needs, to satisfy their wants, to achieve their objectives— that is, trying to solve their "basic economic problem." But it is only in the fleeting moments of recent history that people have made progress in improving their economic conditions. This recent change, once touched off, turned out to be *explosive.* And you who are lucky (or unlucky?) enough to be living today were born right into the middle of this blast.

Much that will happen during your lifetime will be incomprehensible to you unless you have some awareness and understanding of this explosive change we're all caught up in. In just your short lifetime you have observed rapid changes in so many things—attitudes toward acquiring wealth, toward the environment, toward minority groups; feelings about authority and freedom, about poverty, marriage, sex, education, music, dancing, purpose in life. And you have seen so many new ways of doing things, new productive processes and technology, the computer revolution—so many, many changes! The world of today is already a very different place from the world of yesterday—the world into which *you* were born.

I don't know if it's possible for a person who has lived only about one-fifth of a century to fully grasp this explosive rate of change—this tidal wave sweeping us, hurtling us on into our unknown future. But I'm going to try to give you an overview of what's been happening. Many things will make a lot more sense to you if you understand the rapid changes which have been and are occurring—changes caused, to a very large extent, by changes in the economic *conditions* and the economic *behavior* of mankind, and by changes in mankind's *philosophies* about economics.

How Rapidly Time Passes!

How quickly the years (even the centuries!) go by. You have not yet lived long enough to observe the passing of very much time, so it may be difficult for you to develop an awareness of how rapidly time passes—especially historical time.

If you are twenty years old you have lived one-fifth of a century—perhaps one-fourth of your lifetime. During the other three-fourths of your life, time will seem to go by much more rapidly than during the first one-fourth. And after the other three-fourths go by, all your time will have passed. You see, a human lifetime really isn't very long. Historically speaking, one lifetime, or even one century, is a very short time. After all, you have already "lived up" a fourth of a lifetime and a fifth of a century!

If you can realize the speed at which time passes you may be able to feel the explosive rate of change in our world of the 1970s. It was only about *two centuries ago* that the United States was established as a nation. That's less than three complete lifetimes. It was *three centuries before that* when Columbus discovered America. But it was *ten centuries before that* when the Roman Empire collapsed, and some *thirty-five centuries before that* when the early civilizations were emerging in Babylonia and the Nile Valley. And before that, for how long had man already been on the earth? *More than ten thousand centuries!*

Explosive Change Is Being Fueled by Economic Factors

Today's explosion isn't entirely an economic explosion. (Nothing in the real world is *entirely* economic, of course.) But economic factors are providing much force to the blast. Without the disruptive influence of adventuresome and acquisitive individuals, breaking free, following the market, struggling to enrich themselves and simultaneously enriching future generations—without all this, the explosive thrust of the modern world wouldn't have developed. So if you are going to understand what is happening to you, to your world, now, in your lifetime—if you are going to be able to see the explosion in which you are caught, hurtling along, mostly out of control—if you are to gain any idea of where all this might be going, and why, and how—then you must be able to see and understand the economic forces at work.

It isn't that understanding the economic forces of change will let you see with any certainty where the world is going. It won't. But at least it will help you to understand that you are caught up in a world of explosive change. You will be able to understand a little better what's happening to all of us, and how, and why, and perhaps you'll gain some insight into where it all *might* be going. If you get all that out of reading this little book, then surely your time will have been well spent.

1

THE SLOW EVOLUTION OF TRADITIONAL ECONOMIC LIFE—FROM ANCIENT TIMES TO THE INDUSTRIAL REVOLUTION

After Thousands of Centuries of Very Little Change,
Economic Forces Suddenly Trigger an Explosion and
Everyone Is Caught in the Force of the Blast

Let's go back to an earlier time—to a time when things were going along in a sort of changeless pattern—a time before all this rapid change began. Let's see how things were then, and what was going on. Then we'll talk about what happened—what made the whole thing blow up.

THE ECONOMICS OF ANCIENT TIMES

Man has been on earth for more than ten thousand centuries. But it was only about fifty centuries ago that "civilizations" began to emerge.

The Cradles of Civilization

Historians talk about the "cradles of civilization": Mesopotamia, Babylonia, the Nile Valley—all places you have heard about many times. In Asia there were still other early civilizations, some even older and perhaps more advanced than those of the Middle East. In all these places, people always faced their economic problem—how to deal with scarcity, how to choose what to do with the limited things they had: What to use? And what to save? What to make? And who will get how much of what?

Each of the ancient societies had to have some kind of economic system—some way of getting the choices made and the decisions carried out. And what system? Like all economic systems, some mixture of social, political, and market forces or processes. But the choices in the ancient societies were made and carried out mostly by the social force of *tradition,* as influenced and altered in various ways from time to time by the political force of *command.*

Some trade existed, but very little. Trade had almost no influence on the life patterns of the people. Usually, people produced for themselves and shared with their families and leaders. Sometimes the force of command by the ruler—sheik or pharoah or some such—would turn people into slaves and exert a powerful influence on the society's economic choices. (Certainly the pyramids were not built in response to the free wishes of the common people!)

Ancient Greece and Rome

From the cradles of civilization we can leap forward about twenty-five centuries to the early days of Greece and Rome—at about the time of Confucius and Buddha in Asia, about five centuries before the birth of Christ. And what do we find that was different? Actually, not very much. There had been a good bit of social and political evolution. Specialization and trade were somewhat more developed. People had learned how to do and make a lot more things. But the economic systems were still mostly tradition-bound. Workers, craftsmen, noblemen, slaves, all followed in the footsteps of their fathers—the traditional way. Except when conquerors would come in, take rule, and use the force of command to make changes, the economic choices of production and distribution followed traditional patterns century after century.

This same pattern of rule by tradition was followed in the early civilizations of India, China and Japan. Ruling families came and went, kingdoms and empires waxed and waned, but customs and traditions controlled most aspects of people's lives. Economic allocations were determined by the customs of society—that is, by the social system. By tradition.

In the twenty-five centuries between the early civilizations and the rise of the Greek and Roman city-states, the economic systems—the ways of solving the basic economic problem, making the economic choices—really didn't change much. Some changes would occur in one place or another from time to time. But the movement was mostly back and forth. There wasn't much continuous progress—no step-by-step evolution of new and better ways of solving the society's economic problem; no cumulative chain reaction of economic progress from one solution of the problem to an improved solution.

From time to time, political control over the economy would be more powerful in one place or another. But as time passed, the rulers (the "government") would change, government directives would be relaxed, and tradition again would take over. Throughout these many centuries the economic choices generally reflected the traditions of the society, but as modified by the waxing and waning of political controls.

Under the early Greek and Roman civilizations there was some economic (as well as social and political) progress. Some markets were developing and expanding. The market forces of demand, supply, and price were having some influence on the production and distribution choices of the society—but still only very little. Almost all of the choices were either preordained by tradition or ordered by command. The same was true of the civilizations of the Far East. Societies were essentially agrarian; most people were peasants, earning their subsistence from the land. Many members of the "labor force" were slaves, serving and carrying out the economic choices of their rich and powerful masters; many were soldiers, serving and carrying out the economic choices of those who held the political powers of the state.

Early Ideas on Economics

As you know, during the days of ancient Greece and Rome philosophers were trying to understand and explain things. The most outstanding of them was Aristotle. While Aristotle was becoming "the father" of almost every science—astronomy, chemistry, psychology, biology, medicine, geology, and others—economics did not escape his scrutiny. He expressed some very definite thoughts about economics. Would you believe that Aristotle's ideas about economics set the tenor of Western economic thought for the next *ten centuries?* That's a fact.

Aristotle's Economic Philosophy. Aristotle's economic philosophy was ideal for maintaining stability and harmony and social justice in a tradition-bound society. In such societies, flexibility and change would be disruptive and socially undesirable. But for a society which has broken the bonds of tradition—a society which is responding to the powerful forces of the market—Aristotle's economic teachings would not fit. Yet even today we find fragments of Aristotle's economic thought lingering in the minds of many people in the world. So let's take a minute to look at some of the things he said.

Aristotle considered exchange and borrowing and lending money to be unproductive activities. Each person (or family) should produce what he needs for himself. If someone happens to have a surplus he may exchange it or sell it to someone else for a "just" price. But it isn't good for one person to buy something with the idea of reselling it to someone else at a profit. The middleman-trader is detrimental to the society because he buys for *less* than the "just price" and/or sells for *more* than the "just price." That must be true, otherwise he would make no profit! So he is a parasite on the society. He enriches himself at the expense of others.

Even worse than the middleman-traders, according to Aristotle, were those who would lend money and charge interest. Interest is usury—an unjust charge. Since people can't actually make things with money (as they can with machines and raw materials, etc.) money is not productive. Therefore anyone who lends money should not expect to get back any more than the amount he lent.

Early Religious Writings on Economics. Aristotle was not the first to write on economics. There were many before him. Economic thoughts have been included in the writings of most philosophers from the very beginning. The Old Testament and New Testament of the Bible contain much economics, as do the writings of religions other than Christianity. Every religion has been concerned with the issues of the right and wrong economic behavior, and with social choices.

The economic question, "How to do the best for our people with the limited things available," has been a central one for every religion. The Bible, the Talmud, the Koran, and other sacred scriptures and religious writings contain much economic thought. The concepts of what is right and what is wrong in economic matters, of sharing, of just price, of work and leisure—all these have been matters of concern for religious and moral philosophers as far back as recorded history can take us (and very likely even before that).

One Person's Gain Is Another's Loss. The basic ideas of Aristotelian economic thought were reflected in the economic philosophies of early Christianity. The most outstanding economic writer among the many medieval Christian philosophers was St. Thomas Aquinas. His writings on economics emphasize the idea of "just price" and go into great detail on the injustices of lending money for interest, and of trading for profit. The concepts of trading, working to get ahead, acquiring material wealth—all the conditions essential for the market process to operate and to stimulate economic growth—were condemned by the medieval Christian writers.

It was not considered moral to acquire things and to try to enrich one's self. Underlying this anti-acquisitive attitude was the idea that there was only so much of wealth and things around. Any person who worked to acquire more would be forcing others to get by with less. That was bad. A good, moral person would deny himself things, be charitable, give his things to others.

It wasn't that the religious (and other) philosophers wanted everybody to be poor and miserable. Not at all! The hard economic facts of life required that almost all of the people be poor almost all of the time, anyway. So, better to be purposefully poor and feel good about it than to be accidentally poor and be miserable! Also, consider this: Poor people (and poor families and poor tribes) never get murdered for their possessions! And there was a lot of that going on in those days.

The highest form of "economic morality" was to live in poverty, consuming very little and leaving almost everything for others. The idea of economic growth—of people working out ways to become more productive; of each person producing more and thereby enriching both himself and society—that idea wouldn't be understood and accepted until many centuries later. In the traditional societies and in some religions it is still not accepted, even in the world of the 1970s.

For anything as inescapable as the economic problem, you might know that many people would have been thinking and talking and moralizing about it ever since the beginning of time. But now let's take a look at what was going on in the world back when the Greek and Roman city-states were being replaced by the Roman Empire, at about the time of Christ.

The Roman Empire

The early civilizations of Greece and Rome began some five centuries before the time of Christ and continued until about his time. Then the Roman Empire began and continued for about five centuries after Christ. Under the Roman Empire the political force of command took control over many of the economic choices. The government decided about the uses of many resources and about the activities of many people. Many of the social forces of tradition were pushed aside.

Great changes were made in the organization of economic activity and in the choices as to what was to be produced and how it was to be shared among the people. As the Romans spread out over the land, they changed the ways the resources and the energies of the people were used. They redirected and forced increases in productive activities. Using the force of command, they generated increased outputs and held down consumption, created *forced savings* and generated the surpluses needed to support the administrators, the soldiers, and the idle rich, and also to make "investments"—in military equipment, roads, buildings, and whatever else those who held the political power wanted the "savings" to be invested in.

Command Generated Progress

Here's an interesting point: Throughout all of ancient and medieval history and until capitalism emerged (only recently), economic progress—savings going into investment and bringing economic growth—rarely occurred except under the impetus of command. In the ancient societies there always seems to have been an elite group running things, living high, and ordering other people around. And always lots of slaves. Most of what we call the advance of civilization—in the arts, in knowledge and philosophy, in buildings, roads, port facilities—all seem to have been brought about by government command, exercised by one or a few forceful rulers.

Traditional systems are designed for survival. Because they seek stability they impede change. So until the force of the market process (only recently) began to wield its influence, progress had to depend on the redirecting influences of powerful political forces. People had to be ordered around. Could it have been otherwise? As long as people follow the social process of tradition, the society is maintained—but that's all. The society remains stationary. All the output is consumed; no economic growth occurs.

Through the force of command the people can be made to produce more and consume less. Surpluses can be generated and economic progress can result. That's the way it happened in the early civilizations, and in the Roman Empire. It is happening that way in several places in the world even today. But on with our story.

THE MEDIEVAL PERIOD

During the fifth century AD, the Roman Empire came to an end. The administrative ties, the communications and controls which held all the outlying units of the empire together, just sort of dissolved. Each of the outlying regions was left free to go its own way. In some localities Germanic peoples took over control from the Romans, but before long in most localities the people were just left alone to go their own way. Without the controls, laws, and productive activities directed (commanded) by the Romans, each little locality sort of slipped back to a traditional, subsistence economic system.

The Emergence of Feudalism

Little separate, independent socio-economic-political units emerged throughout Europe. As time passed, the ties that held together the larger of the little units dissolved. The result: more and more smaller and smaller units. Different activities and patterns of behavior emerged in different places. In most places there was a general breakdown of laws. People had to figure out their own ways of protecting themselves. There was almost no trade or commerce. Throughout most of Western Europe there evolved the economic, social, and political arrangement we call *feudalism.*

You have already heard many times about feudalism. It took a variety of forms. You know that it was a kind of "mutual responsibility" arrangement. The "lord of the manor" was supposed to protect the people from wandering bands of thieves and plunderers. In exchange, the people had to work to support the manor. The serfs worked the land to produce food, and made the implements and other things needed to keep the little economy going. Each person had his job to do and each was allowed his meager share of the output.

The serfs were sort of slaves. They weren't free to leave, and they were bound to do the bidding of their lord. Still, customs and traditions placed some limits on the lord's power to run the lives of his serfs. For example, serfs weren't usually bought and sold, and usually they were allowed some land rights and some chance to produce things for themselves. The serfs lived much better on some manors than on others, of course. It depended a lot on the attitude and the wisdom of the one who held the political power— that is, on the lord of the manor.

This variety of feudalistic economic-social-political arrangements evolved during the centuries after the end of the Roman Empire and continued to exist for about ten centuries—up to about the time Columbus discovered America. Each century saw some change, but usually not very much. Most of the changes were just back and forth— not cumulative, progressive changes. There was very little trade and commerce. Usually the obstacles were too great.

Some of the Italian trading cities—Venice and Genoa especially—and some in Flanders and elsewhere managed to do all right. But eventually, as the centuries passed, little by little some *cumulative, progressive* changes did begin to creep in. Very slowly at first, and then more rapidly, some chain-reactions were getting started. Some of the changes began to set the stage for the destruction of the stable, tradition-bound feudal way of life. But before we get into that, here's a little more about the economics of medieval times.

What Kind of Economic System Is Feudalism?

Suppose someone asked you what kind of economic system existed in Western Europe during this period of ten centuries, between the time that Rome fell to pieces and the time that Columbus discovered America. What would you say? First you would admit that there was much diversity from one place to another and from one time to another. Then you would be quite safe in saying that the thousand-year period was characterized by the existence of many small, tradition-bound socio-political-economic units. As the centuries passed, feudalism became the dominant form of these tradition-bound units. Then as the ten-century period neared its end, feudalism began to crumble. Without knowing it, the world began getting itself ready for the emergence of modern times.

Feudalism really isn't an economic system. It's a situation in which there isn't any "nationwide" economic system. There isn't any "nation," really—just a lot of little independent political-economic units (little socio-political-economic systems), each operating almost entirely on its own. All these little political-economic systems scattered over the face of the British Isles and Western Europe, some much larger than others, some much more enslaved by ruthless masters than others, some having many more ties with the king, or with surrounding feudal estates than others—each different in several respects from the others, each an individual unit—this was feudalism. (To some extent throughout Asia, but especially in Japan, similar patterns of feudalism emerged, quite independently of what was going on in the Western world.)

The Economics of Feudalism

How were the economic choices made on each feudal manor? Tradition was the controlling force, but command was important, too. Almost all of the production and distribution choices were determined by the rules of the society, but as interpreted, enforced, and sometimes modified by the lord of the manor. People were bound to the manor where they were born. They produced the things they were supposed to produce—usually the things their fathers before them had produced—and they received their traditionally · established just shares of the food and other things.

Some trading was going on, to be sure. People bought, sold, and traded things, but usually tradition established the just price for each transaction. The market process—the driving force of demand—was a very minor, almost negligible influence on the production and distribution patterns in the society.

During this period the Roman Catholic Church was a unifying and stabilizing influence. The teachings of the Church emphasized the importance of continuity, of stability, of following the established social, economic, and political traditions. No one was supposed to try to break loose, to get ahead. If he did he would only be hurting others. This life was to be accepted. Preparing for the *next* life was what *really* mattered. Yet somehow, as the centuries passed, change began to creep in. The system began to erode. Ultimately the stage was set for the destruction of this stable socio-economic-political arrangement which had lasted for so many centuries. How easily it might have lasted for many more centuries! But it didn't.

Except for the cumulative series of events which burst the dike and brought the tidal wave of change, we might all now be living on little feudal estates. Maybe I would be your lord—or maybe you, mine! But under the pressure of change, feudalism began crumbling—slowly eroding away. Finally it was swept away. What happened? What touched off the chain reaction—the cumulative series of events which were to destroy the feudal way of life—the end to stable, tradition-bound feudal society?

The Slow Death of Feudalism

Just as feudalism didn't spring up suddenly, it didn't disappear suddenly. The erosive influences were grinding away at it for several centuries. Near the end, the pace of change was quickening. Various forces for change were re-enforcing each other. The chain reaction was beginning. Change was in the wind. Here are some highlights of what happened.

The Crusades. One of the earliest and most continual erosive influences was the Crusades. The Crusades—the "holy wars"—started at the end of the eleventh century and continued, off and on, for some four centuries—until about the time Columbus discovered America. The Crusades were going on when Genghis Khan and Kublai Khan were dashing about with their armies, conquering most of Asia, and when Marco Polo made his famous 25 year long trip to China.

The Crusades had an important "how you gonna keep 'em down on the farm after they've seen Paree" effect. Just as some do now, people then found it easy to live at bare subsistence and to follow custom and tradition if they didn't know of any other kind of life. But once people saw and experienced new and different, more and better things, they were no longer satisfied with things as they were.

Aspirations and feudalism didn't mix. Just as today, aspirations and the traditional societies don't mix. I suppose if there is any one key to the end of feudalism it would be aspirations—the desire for more and better things, and perhaps for more freedom—and the awareness that such things may be possible.

Today, some economists refer to "the revolution of rising expectations" among the people in the less-developed countries. Aspirations are bringing the rapid destruction of these stable, tradition-bound (semi-feudalistic) societies today, right before our eyes! Even in such advanced nations as the United States, Canada, and those of Western Europe, the urban poor and the people in the depressed rural regions refuse to placidly accept their fate. When people see or hear about better conditions, they *want* better conditions.

Fairs, Traveling Merchants, Growing Cities. The Crusades were not the only window to the outside world. There were fairs and traveling merchants. Even cities were beginning to grow up in several places in the British Isles and on the continent—hundreds of small but slowly growing settlements. The cities grew as centers for specialized production and for trade. Some of the adventuresome people were breaking loose from the feudal manors and were going to the towns or traveling with the merchants. Some went to work on ships as trade between the port cities expanded. More and more, people were breaking their feudal ties.

Countries Were Emerging. As the Middle Ages wore on, nation-states (countries, or kingdoms) were growing, becoming more powerful. Most of the feudal manors had been under the jurisdiction of some king all along, but these kingdoms existed in name only. Also, the Byzantine Empire of the Eastern Mediterranean and the Holy Roman Empire of Western Europe had claimed jurisdiction over large areas for many centuries. But so far as the day-to-day matters of living were concerned, these "empires" usually had little or no influence.

In the later centuries of the medieval period, some of the kings began to develop the power to maintain law and protect the people throughout their kingdoms. Travel became safer, and trade, easier. Cities could more easily flourish and grow. Business could be conducted more regularly, more dependably, more safely.

Exploration and World Trade. As the nation-states became stronger and travel increased and cities grew, there were more fairs, more traveling merchants, more shipping and trade. Markets were developing here and there. There were many voyages of exploration. Gold and silver were becoming more plentiful and more widely used as money. These new developments were providing more opportunities for people to escape from their feudal bonds, and more and more of them did.

Enclosures of Common Land. While some of the people were trying to sneak away from the feudal manors, others were being pushed off the land. Traditionally, much of the land (especially in Britain) had been available for common use. This common land was important to many serfs for their subsistence. But as the population expanded, more and more land was enclosed—the land was fenced in by the lords and the common users were fenced off. The enclosures didn't make common users happy. Some fences were torn down from time to time, but the enclosures continued. More and more of the common land was becoming private property, with "no trespassing." Remember what it was like in the "Old West" when the homesteaders came and started fencing in the open range? That's sort of the way it was from time to time and from place to place in late medieval Europe.

The enclosure movement began as far back as the twelfth century and continued (sometimes rapidly, sometimes slowly) for more than seven centuries—through the nineteenth century. As the enclosure movement proceeded, those who had previously used the common lands were forced to move elsewhere. Many of them moved to the towns to seek jobs or some other means of staying alive.

The Increasing Use of Money. With the land enclosures pushing on some of the people and the attractions of the growing towns pulling on others, the towns grew. Trade and money became more and more a part of everyday life for more and more people.

Gold and silver had served as money far back into history. But even in the years when England and the other Western European countries were emerging from feudalism, there were many people who had never seen a gold coin. Then, as feudalism continued to erode, more and more aspects of life began to be related to money. More people began to produce things, not for subsistence but for sale. The market forces of demand, supply, and price were beginning to direct more of the economic choices of the society.

What we are watching is the slow crumbling of the rigid structure of feudalism and the gradually increasing role of the market forces in directing the economic life of society. But the ethics of medieval times didn't approve of letting the market forces run things. So what happened? Soon that problem got itself worked out, too. Here's how.

The Protestant Ethic. Remember what the Christian philosopher, St. Thomas Aquinas, had said about not being acquisitive, not producing and trading for profit, about just price, and about not charging interest (usury) and all that? How can the market forces direct the economic choices unless people are trying to *acquire,* to get ahead by producing something that other people want to buy? The market forces can't work unless people are producing and working to earn more money!

That "don't acquire" philosophy of the Church was really a drag. But then it happened that the opposite philosophy burst forth. The Protestant Reformation occurred just in time to justify the emerging market forces. The one person most responsible for the new philosophy was John Calvin. The philosophy was, of course, *Calvinism.* You can find some of the philosophy of Calvinism buried deep in the teachings of most of the Protestant churches.

According to the medieval Catholic Church, anyone who would produce and trade for the purpose of enriching himself would be doing wrong. But now, suddenly, in the mid-1500s John Calvin offers the world a new economic philosophy—the Protestant Ethic: Work hard. Stay busy. Be thrifty. Save. "The Idle Mind is the Devil's Workshop." Produce a lot and get wealthy. You will produce a lot for yourself, and for your society, too. That will show the world that you are a godly person! That was quite a switch, right?

As Calvin and his followers were spreading the word, the Spanish explorers were over in Mexico and Central and South America relieving the local inhabitants of their gold and silver and bringing it back to Europe—just in case more money might be needed. Somehow the pieces were beginning to fit together. It looks like the market forces of demand, supply, and price are going to get a chance to have their day after all!

The Cumulative Effect of the Erosive Forces

The many changes, the erosive forces we have been talking about, were chipping away at the frozen structure of feudal society for more than five centuries. I'm sure that for a long time it wasn't clear to anyone that anything very different was going on. But the worms were in the woodwork. It was just a matter of time. The erosive forces were at work.

As the centuries passed, the forces for change began speeding up. By the time of John Calvin and the Spanish Conquistadores, irreparable damage to the old social order had already been done. Many cities had emerged as centers of economic life, with money, and trade, and each with its own set of customs and rules—its own ways of doing things. Life in the emerging cities was distinctly different from the traditional ways of feudal society. City dwellers couldn't be farmers! They had to depend on production and trade for their living.

The slow, steady growth of these urban producing and trading centers resulted in the development of "the city" as a new form of socio-political-economic unit—a new kind of little political and economic system. Each city had its own developing customs and traditions—its ways of doing things. But the newly developing "traditional ways" of the cities were designed to accept and respond to market forces. Then, as trade expanded, the cities were ready to play an ever-increasing role in the economic life of the society.

In the sixteenth century the pace of change in the Western world was beginning to speed up a little. But in Asia the traditional ways of life continued. No cumulative chain reactions of economic progress were touched off in India, China, or Japan. The peoples of Asia, just like those of Africa and the Americas, were unwittingly waiting to fall under the domination of the progressing, progress-hungry, profit-seeking Westerners.

At first, the economic progress of the Western world was slow. Even after America had been discovered, it would be yet another three centuries before the forces of the market process—supply and demand and prices—would really thrust aside the restrictive, rigid forces of tradition and claim control over most of the economic choices of society. But three hundred years had to pass before the world would be ready for the Industrial Revolution.

During this three-hundred-year interlude between the discovery of America and the beginning of the Industrial Revolution the world was unknowingly preparing itself. Money was becoming more and more important. The expanding nation-states were trying to increase their national power. They exercised tight controls over economic activities and trade. The economic policies and philosophies which dominated this transitional period are called *mercantilism.*

MERCANTILISM

The basic idea of mercantilism was that the government directs the economy so as to gain more national wealth and power. More national wealth and power was usually thought of as "more gold and silver." Many of the production and distribution choices were made by the political process—by the king and the nobility. The government would (a) stimulate the output of goods which could be exported in exchange for gold, and (b) limit domestic consumption, both of exportable goods and of imported goods. (The people must not be allowed to overeat, or own many things. Only kings and noblemen should.)

Every king knew that if he had enough gold he could hire enough soldiers, buy enough armaments, and build enough ships to be the most powerful king in the world. He could send out many explorers and privateers, and get back even more gold. Gold was seen as the key to the nation's wealth and power. The economic condition of the average person was not a matter of much concern to those who were making the economic choices for the society under mercantilism.

Mercantilism Imposed Strict Economic Controls

In a word, then, mercantilism was a closely controlled economy, aimed at maximizing exports so as to maximize the inflow of gold. Imports of raw materials were good, because these would go into more manufactured goods for export. It was okay to import cotton, make shirts and skirts, then export the shirts and skirts to trade for more cotton—and for gold. But imports of consumer goods "for the people to enjoy" (like wheat, to eat) was discouraged. Exporting industries were favored in various ways. Imports were restricted.

Does gold make a nation wealthy? Or powerful? If we're thinking in medieval terms, it does. In the days of the feudal kingdoms, gold was power because with gold you could buy those things necessary to be powerful. But when things are exported in exchange for gold, the people have to make do with less. Obviously. So, from the point of view of the rulers and wealthy merchants of the nation, the nation with the greatest inflow of gold would be gaining the most wealth and power. But in terms of the welfare of the people, the greater the gold inflow, the less "wealthy" the nation would be—the fewer things (food, clothing, etc.) would be available for the people.

Competitive National Self-Enrichment

What was happening? The emerging nations were grabbing at the new opportunities and trying to use them to play the old "national power" game, by the old medieval, feudal rules. The very conditions which were bringing the end to feudalism offered the opportunity for the emerging nations to engage in "competitive mercantilism." But mercantilism was based on the idea of every nation getting rich and powerful at the expense of every other nation. The ultimate objective was national wealth and power—not of the *people* (of course not!) but of the few who were running things. And the wealth and power were judged by the old medieval, feudal criteria: gold and military might.

Under mercantilism, each nation should establish colonies, to provide guaranteed sources of raw materials. With these raw materials the nations should produce things, then sell the things back to the colonies and to anyone else who will buy and pay with gold. It might be an overstatement to say that the American Revolution came as a result of the mercantilist policies of England during the 1700s. But certainly British mercantilism was an aggravating factor.

When we look back, mercantilism may not seem to make much sense. But if you can picture the tenor of the times, you can understand it. It was partly medieval, partly "modern world." And as with so many things, once the competition began, once everyone else was a mercantilist, no one could afford to be anything else. Various forms and shades of mercantilism persisted for about three centuries. We still hear mercantilist utterings from time to time right now, in the 1970s. And what about all that gold, first dug out of the ground and refined, then traded for goods, then reburied in the ground at Fort Knox? We still do strange things. (More on that later.)

For almost three centuries—from soon after the discovery of America to the time of the American Revolution—mercantilism was the name of the game. The British, the French, Dutch, Spaniards, Portuguese, Italians, and some others all tried to do whatever they could to increase the "wealth of the nation"—the nation's gold. The rulers and merchants of each nation worked together, playing their own little game, trying to enrich themselves, their nation—both at the expense of all the other nations, and at the expense of their own common people and their colonists as well. This idea, "There's only so much wealth around, so more for me means less for you," was still accepted as a basic truth. The world was not yet ready to accept the idea that there might be economic growth, with a growing amount of total wealth for everybody.

It is easy to look back at mercantilism and criticize this hangover of medieval psychology. But we can forgive them. Even today we can see several medieval hangovers still alive in the modern world. Powerful nation-states still wage medieval wars (using modern weapons) and everyone knows that *everyone* will lose. No one can win in such a conflict! Yet wars persist. Nations keep building weapons. And so long as military power is the name of the game, no nation seems to have any choice but to play it that way. This is one of the sad realities of our moment in history. But we are in the midst of an explosion, remember? We should expect to find fragments and chunks from the pre-explosion period hurtling with us through time. And so we do.

A Three-Hundred-Year Transition

All the time mercantilism was controlling things, trying to hold down consumption, control trade, limit imports, and all that, the conditions for the market economy to emerge—or rather *explode*—were getting set. During this three hundred years of mercantilism—of exploration, colonization, urbanization, the increasing use of money, and the emergence of prices as economic incentives—all this time the conditions were being laid for the real explosion. Quietly, almost without notice and certainly without plan, came the Industrial Revolution. As a small fire in the low grass begins creeping and nobody notices until suddenly it reaches the tall brush and then the trees and then the forest and all is out of control—like that came the Industrial Revolution. Let's talk about that.

THE INDUSTRIAL REVOLUTION

The Industrial Revolution destroyed the traditional ways of doing things. It destroyed the traditional ways of making the economic choices. It blasted away the previous way of life and brought a new one which was for some much better, for others much worse. But for everybody it was different. We, today, are still in the midst of the explosion which was touched off by the Industrial Revolution. We are hurtling along at a dizzying pace—and the pace seems to be picking up all the time. No wonder things are confused these days!

The Industrial Revolution gave the capitalist industrialists the opportunity to hire the displaced peasants. There were many workers looking for jobs. Wages were low. The new machine production was much more efficient than the hand-tool production of the craftsman. Output per worker was high; businesses made big profits. With the high profits, the capitalist-industrialists bought more machinery. They built more factories, produced more goods, and made even more profits, built even more factories. On and on went the process of industrialization. Faster and faster and faster. The early thrust of the Industrial Revolution was in England, in the textile industry. From there it spread to other places and to other industries. You've heard all the names of the famous inventors and their famous gadgets— from John Kay and his "flying shuttle" (about 1750) to Hargreaves' "spinning jenny" (about 1770) and to Eli Whitney's "cotton gin" (about 1790). By 1800 the output per man had increased greatly in the textile industry. Much more cloth was being made, and the demand for cotton and wool was expanding rapidly. The increased demand and the higher prices made cotton growing and sheep raising very profitable.

In the United States, Southern plantation owners got rich, bought more slaves, cleared more land, planted more cotton, and got richer. In England the landlords speeded up their enclosures of land, forced the peasants off, turned the lands into grazing pastures for sheep—and got rich. The peasants went to the cities where jobs in the textile mills were available. More and more of the pieces were fitting together. Labor and land and capital were responding to demand. The automatic market forces were really beginning to direct and control society's scarce resources.

Market Forces Begin to Direct Production

With the breakdown of the traditional uses for resources—for land, labor, and capital—the owners of these "factors of production" began to sell their factors to the highest bidders. For example, before the enclosures, land was just land, available for common use. After the enclosure of a piece of land, that land became a person's private property. The owner would use the land the best way he could, to bring him the biggest return he could get. Once the land became enclosed private property, it became a "responsive factor of production," ready to do the bidding of the forces of the market—of demand, and prices.

In the case of labor, as long as tradition gives each person his occupation and his station in life, he is not available to "sell his labor" in response to the market's demands. But after a person gets pushed off the land, with no money and no source of food, his labor suddenly becomes very responsive to the market forces of demand, and prices. He looks for a job anywhere he can get a *price* (wage, or salary) for his labor. *Market forces* begin to direct his labor. This transition wasn't always pleasant for the person involved. But for the productivity of the economic system, and the growth which was about to happen—growth which would bring freedom from want to so many people in future generations—the long-run benefit of the transition was undeniable.

Back in history, whenever the traditional society was to be induced to do things differently—to get people to produce more things and consume less, or to move from one kind of activity to another—the political process (government command) usually was required to bring about the change. But here, as the Industrial Revolution is getting going, we see *market forces* directing more and more people and things. *Desire for reward* is replacing fear of punishment as the motive force driving the common man.

There are major shifts in both the production and distribution choices in the society. And notice this: The political process does not need to be involved at all! In fact, quite the opposite. The unleashed forces of the market are exercising their great power, wresting the economic choice-making functions both from the traditional heritages of the society and from the political control of the kings and nobles. The "natural process of the market" is moving the factors of production (land, labor, capital) into different uses, causing the factors to respond to the *market demands* of the society. And production is expanding in a way that never happened before in the history of the world!

Market Forces Generate Economic Growth

Capitalist industrialists were making big profits. With their profits they bought more machines, built more factories, caused all kinds of capital goods to be produced. More factors of production flowed into making more capital. More and better kinds of factories and machines were being built. This was the process of economic growth in action. This is what was really happening.

This rapid growth process was going on in the later 1700s and throughout the 1800s and on into the present century. This is the process which built the industrial base for the economically advanced nations. It's because of this economic growth process that most of us in the advanced nations are enjoying so much freedom of choice, so much leisure time, such easy working conditions, and so many products and services—warm houses, fast cars, medical attention, and all that. But more about the Industrial Revolution.

The World Socio-Economic Upheaval of the 1800s

The big thrust of industrial growth in the world didn't really get going until the early 1800s. By that time steel had been developed, and the bugs had been worked out of the steam engine. Now better machinery could be built and driven by steam power. Then came the steamboat, the railroads, and the telegraph. By the mid 1800s, not just Great Britain, but all of Europe and the United States were undergoing the violently disruptive impact of rapid industrialization.

During the 1800s, centuries of social tradition were ripped apart. This was the period which rang the death knell on a way of life. It marked the beginning of another way of life—one of continual, explosive change. It was during this time that in the United States, in a few short decades, "the West was won." And it was during this time that in Europe, Friedrich Engels helped a bitter and impoverished Karl Marx as they wrote the *Communist Manifesto* calling for and predicting the end of capitalism. You'll hear more about that later.

It isn't much of an overstatement to say that during the 1800s the entire society of the industrializing part of the world restructured itself—physically, geographically, socially, economically. People bred like rabbits. The growing population moved toward the industrial centers—toward the coal and iron deposits—and along the expanding railroads, to the seaports, the transportation and trade centers—and to the United States and Canada. Some poor people got very rich. But most of them just moved somewhere else, got jobs, worked hard, and stayed poor.

Most working people in most places were living under miserable conditions. Were they miserable? Who can say? Perhaps they accepted their fate in the same way that most of the people of the world always have had to accept their fate. Hunger has been the "natural condition" of most people in the world, in the traditional societies, much of the time. In the 150-year period of rapid socio-economic turmoil between 1750 and 1900, many people looked very miserable. Their meager possessions, their lack of opportunity to get ahead, the many, many hours they had to work just to keep going certainly didn't give them much time or cause to be happy.

Traditional Patterns Were Stripped Away

What was happening? Suddenly people were no longer being cared for by the traditional social processes. A person no longer had his niche in society as he had had in feudal times. The "social security" of traditional society was gone. Everything was changing. It was a new ball game.

Suddenly people were living in a world in which they had no choice but to take care of themselves. A person received his income (and his "distributive share" of the output) on the basis of what "factors of production" he had to sell. If someone did not have any land or capital, he had to sell his labor. So that's just what he did. As Bob Dylan would say, "the times they were a-changin'." The Industrial Revolution was in progress and the market process was taking control of society's economic choices. People and things were being shifted suddenly—yesterday suddenly thrust into tomorrow.

Who likes to see the former peasants working in the sweat shops from before sunrise until after sunset? And their children too! While the rich factory owners are making millions, building new factories up and down the valley and living off the fat of the land? Nobody. What a miserable, unjust solution to society's economic problem!

To be sure, the peasant is glad to have the job because it's a way of staying alive. But an economic arrangement which distributes so much of the output (income) to the factory owners and so little to the workers? This is capitalism? Yes, this was the capitalism of these disruptive days of the nineteenth-century Industrial Revolution. The market forces of demand and supply and prices were being unleashed. The *market process* was exerting its influence. Overthrowing tradition. Sidestepping command. A new, powerful, explosive force was being set loose in the world. Yes, it really was a brand new ball game.

Rapid Economic Progress Was Being Made

Anybody who wasn't too concerned about the poverty of the people could see that progress was afoot. More product was being made. More factories being built. More people hired. More output per man. But still, poverty among the masses. Everywhere.

The enclosures continued to spread. More and more people were forced off the common land. They drifted into the cities to seek jobs. Miserable though the jobs were, and miserably low the wages—still, it was a way to survive. In England, the "corn laws" (mercantilist tariffs to limit the import of all kinds of grain) forced high prices for grain and flour and bread and for most other kinds of food eaten by the common people. The high prices kept people from eating very much.

People worked for low wages and had to pay high prices for food. But profits were being made. The landowners were doing very well. The capitalist entrepreneurs were making high profits and investing in more factories and better machinery and equipment. They were doing just fine. And as a result of all this the economy was growing by leaps and bounds.

The Population Explosion

Population was expanding rapidly. After all the thousands of centuries that man has been on earth, and then over the many centuries from the cradles of civilization to the days of the ancient Greeks and Romans, to the Roman Empire and on into the Middle Ages—up to the time of the first of the Crusades (about AD 1100) the population of the world was still only about *300 million people.* By the time Columbus discovered America (only four centuries later) the population of the world had *increased by about 50 percent*—to about *450 million.* Then from 1492 until the time the United States became a nation (only *three centuries later)* the world's population *doubled*—to about *900 million.* Can you see what's happening? It's a population explosion!

But the figures for world population don't really show the seriousness of the true picture. What was going on in Europe? In the places where all this new activity was underway?

During the 1700s—only *one century*—Europe's population *doubled.* And look at this: During the 1800s, England's population expanded from about nine million to thirty-five million—a *fourfold increase!* By 1900 the world's population stood at 1.5 billion. It was destined to double again (to *3 billion)* by 1960, and perhaps to *double again* (to *6 billion)* before the end of the twentieth century. (Now do you wonder why the world suddenly finds that it has a pollution problem? A problem of ecological imbalance? More on that later.)

During the 1700s and 1800s, the rapidly expanding population compounded the human tragedy of poverty—but it supplied labor to support the rapid industrial growth, and markets for the industrial output. There is no question that growth was rapid. Was all this economic growth—this increased industrialization and increased output—the result of the mercantilists' economic controls? Or was some other force at work?

The Challenge to Mercantilism

The mercantilist philosophy of "restrict local consumption, export more goods, get more gold, and make the nation wealthy" was much in evidence. But as the industrial revolution exploded on the scene the voices of others began to be heard—the voices of *the new industrialists.* Many of the industrialists wanted to be free of the government restrictions and regulations of mercantilism. The new industrialists saw the advantages of selling wherever they had the opportunity to sell at the best price, and of buying inputs or whatever else they wanted to buy from wherever they could find them available at the best price—in England, France, Germany, the United States, or wherever.

The industrialists and the mercantilists did not agree. And the humanists who were concerned about the poverty of most of the factory workers in the rapidly expanding cities were not happy with the situation, either. What was going on? Why were conditions as they were? Why was there so much disruption and poverty? What was it all leading to? What should the government be doing? What should anybody be doing? What had gone wrong with the world? Nobody seemed to know.

Historical explosion was beginning. But no one could know that. Everything looked all confused. Not enough cumulative change could be seen to be able to tell what was happening. To many people it must have looked like chaos. Certainly they never could have dreamed of what really was going on. Surely it wasn't easy for anyone to see order or purpose in all that misery and turmoil! Maybe it takes until about now—until the 1970s—for us to be able to look back and see what really was beginning to happen. We can't see where it's all going, even yet. Of course not. Only time will reveal the answer to that question.

Today we can look back over the broad sweep of history and see the cumulative effect of hundreds of years of little, erosive changes—changes which like worms in the woodwork were eating away at the old, stable, traditional social structure and preparing the world for violent change. We can see how the rate of change started speeding up, faster and faster—leading into, supporting, and then being whisked along by the rapid-fire series of new inventions and innovations. The growing factories and machines, the socio-economic disruption, all this turmoil—this is the period we call the Industrial Revolution. It was really the blast-off on this trip that now we all are taking—this trip of explosive change, hurtling us through time, heading at breakneck speed into an unknown future.

How did it look in the late 1700s to the people who were trying to figure out what was going on? There was a lot of human suffering. People disagreed about what was happening. But there was no question that *new things were going on.* Various philosophers, scholars, businessmen, and just ordinary people were trying to figure out what was going on—many were trying to explain and evaluate the situation, perhaps to suggest some way to improve things. Mercantilism had both its proponents and its critics as far back as the 1500s. But during the late 1700s the critics of the government's economic controls of mercantilism were becoming more insistent and more effective.

BEHOLD! THE MARKET PROCESS TAKES OVER

You and I can look back and understand some of what was happening. We can see that the market forces were exerting their influences more and more over the economic choices of the society. The great supply of labor was holding down the wage rate, providing markets for products and keeping profits high. The high profits were providing great stimulation for building capital—for economic growth. But it wasn't easy to look at the rapidly expanding population and all the suffering and confusion and make any sense out of what was going on.

How could they know that the market process—the free market forces of supply and demand—were taking over, automatically directing the economy? They couldn't, of course. Then, in 1776, a new book appeared. It explained the whole thing—all about the automatic operation of the market process, and how it works for the good of everybody.

The book was written by a professor, a Scotsman with an unlikely name: Adam Smith. Professor Adam Smith was not the first to talk about "free market forces" and how they work. But he was the first to pull it all together. He explained the whole process in his big economics book, titled: *An Inquiry into the Nature and Causes of the Wealth of Nations* (usually referred to as *Wealth of Nations*). That's what Adam Smith did. For that he is called "the father of modern economics."

Adam Smith gave the philosophers and the other thinking people of the world a new way to look at what was going on. He gave them a new explanation of what it all meant, where it was all going, and how. We're going to be talking about what Adam Smith had to say. But that discussion, and the discussion of who else said what—the economic ideas of Malthus, Ricardo, Mill, Marshall, Owen, Marx, and others who were trying to make sense out of what was going on in the world—that must wait for the next chapters.

For now, take a few minutes to think about this broad sweep of history leading up to the Industrial Revolution. Then take a few more minutes and try to picture the turmoil the world had gotten itself into. Explosive, cumulative, accelerating economic change, like a tidal wave, was sweeping away the stable social structures of the past and leaving in its wake masses of people struggling for new ways to survive. A world turned upside down—a real "Poseidon Adventure"! And as the people struggled to survive, they followed the pull of the powerful forces of the market—forces which were grasping control, taking over, beginning to direct the economic choices of the society.

2

THE EMERGENCE OF NEW ECONOMIC CONDITIONS, IDEAS, AND THEORIES— THE INDUSTRIAL REVOLUTION (1750s-1850s)

The Classical Economists Tried to
Explain the World and the
Utopian Socialists Tried
To Change It

It was the late 1700s. Hard times were everywhere. What a miserable world! Hungry, cold, sick people. Split up families. Very tedious work. Very long hours. Very low pay. No wonder people were trying to understand the economics of all this. What was going on? Wasn't there some better way? Couldn't something be done? Some new government policies or programs perhaps? Surely life on earth could be made into something better than this! But how? The answers were not easy to find.

The Challenge to Mercantilism

One thing was dawning on an increasing number of people: Mercantilism did not seem to be the answer. You remember that during the Middle Ages and on back into ancient times, the philosophers, religious writers, and concerned citizens of each day and age were commenting on (frequently criticizing) the economic issues of the day. As you might expect, the critical commenting continued throughout the three-hundred-year period of mercantilism. As time went on, mercantilism came more and more under attack.

During the 1700s the mercantilist philosophy suffered some serious blows. The most devastating, as you already may have guessed, came from our perceptive Scottish friend, Professor Adam Smith. But during the mid-1700s (a few decades before Smith's *Wealth of Nations*) some French philosophers were developing a new explanation of what was going on. Before we get into Smith's *Wealth of Nations* we need to say a few words about these French philosophers—the ones we call the *Physiocrats*.

The Physiocrats

The Physiocrats said that it would be better if the government would just leave people alone. They emphasized the economic importance of agricultural production. Only agricultural production created "new things out of nowhere," so to speak. Manufacturing and trade were "sterile" activities. Such activities only moved or changed things. Nothing was really "created."

It was their idea that when people produce from the soil, nature and man are working together. This partnership was necessary to produce more physical output—that is, more real wealth for the nation. They said that mercantilist controls interfered with this process. The term "laissez-faire" comes from the French Physiocrats. As you know, the term means that the government should let each person alone to make his own economic way—to do whatever he wants with his time, energy, resources, capital, and with whatever else he has to work with.

The French Physiocrats called attention to some of the fallacies of mercantilism. Francois Quesnay (frawn-SWA kay-NAY), a leading Physiocrat, developed the concept that economic activity follows a kind of circular flow. His *Tableau Economique* shows that the people of the society produce, then consume some and save some, then produce again. Using what they have saved, they can produce more. Around and around goes the production-consumption circle. Each time, some is saved. The economy grows. This was Quesnay's explanation of *how the nation gains its wealth.*

The Physiocrats attacked the mercantilists by offering a new, different explanation of both the *form* and *source* of the nation's wealth. To the Physiocrats, the nation's wealth was the *physical output* produced from the soil. Government controls only interfered with the wealth-producing process, so the Physiocrats called for a policy of laissez-faire.

To the mercantilists, wealth was the *gold* acquired by selling things. Government controls were called for, to force the people to produce the "right" products and not to consume too much, and to force trade to flow in the "right" directions.

The Physiocrats and the mercantilists disagreed about both (a) the *nature* of a nation's wealth and (b) the *causes* of a nation's wealth. Perhaps now you can understand why Adam Smith chose for his book the title: *An Inquiry into the Nature and Causes of the Wealth of Nations.* You know by now that Smith's book is going to say that the mercantilist concept of the *nature* of wealth is wrong, and that the mercantilist explanation of what *causes* a nation to be wealthy is wrong. You probably also know that Smith is going to explain the automatic operation of the market process—how the forces of free markets (demand, supply, price)—work to bring about the wealthiest nation. Smith's book explains *how* a nation will become wealthiest if it will follow a laissez-faire policy and just let the automatic market process take care of things. That was the real purpose of his book—to make that point. He made the point very well. So well, in fact, that his book had quite an impact on the world and on all future ideas about economics. Let's talk about Adam Smith and his big economics book.

ADAM SMITH AND THE WEALTH OF NATIONS

Adam Smith's historic book was published in the historic year 1776. It offered some comprehensive and plausible answers to the question: "What's going on in this messy, miserable world?" His answers were good. Much of what he said is as true today as it was then.

Adam Smith's book contained a lot of economics. It talked about the advantages of specialization and trade. It talked about savings and investment and economic growth. It explained how the market process automatically gets the "right" things to be produced, how it automatically moves the factors of production to the "right" places to do the "right" things, and how it automatically arranges for the "right" amount of the output to be shared by each person. Truly, *Wealth of Nations* was, and is, an outstanding economics book.

Laissez-Faire and Competition

Wealth of Nations explained how the businessman, trader, industrialist, landowner, worker, or anyone else, in trying to get ahead, would automatically be tricked (by the free market forces) into serving the best interests of the society— by conserving resources, and by producing the right numbers of the right kinds of goods. It worked like this: The person who used his energies and resources to make what the society *wanted most,* would get paid a lot. The businessman who would produce a much-wanted, highly valued product while being careful to conserve society's scarce resources would be doing a great service for society. For this he would be rewarded with big profits. Everyone in the society would have a strong incentive to be productive, so everyone would work hard producing the most valued things. The total product would be great. The nation's wealth would grow more and more. A neat automatic system, right?

Wealth of Nations explained how everything would come out best if the government followed a policy of laissez-faire—that is, if it just kept its hands off and did not interfere with what people were producing or consuming, or with prices, or with anything about the operation of the automatic market process. The book emphasized the essential role of competition, to protect the society against monopolistic sellers or buyers, or groups of sellers or buyers. It explained that "laissez-faire" wouldn't mean economic chaos, because the natural market forces would keep the economy in control and moving in desirable directions. And it explained even more.

Yes, there is much good economics in Smith's book. Also, there is much anti-mercantilism—much argument for individual freedom and against government interference and controls. While Thomas Jefferson in the *Declaration of Independence,* and other philosophers in other writings, were offering the world justification for *political freedom,* Adam Smith was offering the world justification for *economic freedom.*

Nineteenth-Century Liberalism

The *Declaration of Independence* (also, as you know, written in 1776) and the *Wealth of Nations* both reflected their times—the emergence of "nineteenth-century liberalism"—the idea of freedom of the individual, the "inalienable rights" of every man. The United States, a new nation created in the midst of this newly emerging philosophy, still carries a deep commitment to democracy, and to laissez-faire. You can see it in the U.S. political system and economic system. This anti-government philosophy was really strong at the time the United States Constitution was written. Perhaps this helps to explain why the U.S. government for so many years showed such great reluctance to take any action to influence conditions in the economy. Even today, many Americans stand strong against almost any kind of government involvement in the economy.

The Invisible Hand

Adam Smith's book marks the beginning of "classical economics." It tells the world that laissez-faire can work. It explains the market process. It says that if the government leaves the people free to make their own economic choices, each person who seeks to follow his own best interest will be guided "as though by an invisible hand" to do the things which are best for the whole society.

In *Wealth of Nations,* Adam Smith explains how self-interest will drive individuals to do those things which others want them to do. He explains how each person will be financially rewarded for the good things he does for society. He explains how the market process will generate savings and investment and bring economic growth, more output, and more good things for everybody. He explains how a nation which follows laissez-faire will automatically become more wealthy, more powerful, more productive— how the people will enjoy higher standards of living if *market forces* are in control than they would if the *government* tried to control things.

Smith Was Optimistic

Adam Smith thus explained the misery and hardship of England and the Western world in terms which seemed to make it all worthwhile in the long run. He was optimistic. He explained how businessmen making profits would reinvest in more capital to try to make even more profits. The result: more growth, greater production, and (eventually) higher wages and better conditions for the common people.

Adam Smith's work was greatly appreciated by the capitalist industrialists during the hectic days of the Industrial Revolution. *Wealth of Nations* gave them a way to justify their self-serving activities and a respectable explanation for their great wealth and profits. Businessmen could explain that as they were being selfish in seeking profit, they were really working for the good of society. Adam Smith had told them so!

Natural Laws of Economic Behavior

Adam Smith explained a kind of "natural law of economic behavior." If the government followed any policy other than laissez-faire, it would thwart this natural law. The government would keep the economy from working properly. How stupid that would be! Talk about an effective argument against the government controls of mercantilism! With the natural laws of economic behavior controlling things, it made sense to permit individuals to be free to make their own economic choices.

Adam Smith didn't invent the natural laws of the free market. The market process was already there, busily at work. Tradition had already given way to the new order of things. There was a new kind of control over the economic choices—a new kind of influence directing economic life. Smith just showed it to people. He gave them a way to look at and recognize it—a way to understand and explain what was going on. He gave the world the first systematic explanation of how the market process works—of how each individual, working for his own greatest benefit, will automatically bring the greatest benefit to all of society.

His thesis was that the nation will be most wealthy, the people will fare best, if they are left free to follow their own selfish interests. He emphasized the need for free markets, for competition, and for the factors of production to move freely in response to market prices—for each person to produce whatever will bring him the most income.

Division of Labor, Specialization, Trade

Smith emphasized the essential role that trade plays in bringing about the most productive, most efficient uses of the society's resources. He explained the importance of specialization, of division of labor. A jack-of-all trades can't be as productive as one who specializes. But it's obvious that if a person is going to specialize, he must be able to trade his output—to sell it and get some other things in return. Smith emphasized the indisputable fact that specialization requires trade—that only when a producer can trade his output can he specialize.

The Functions of Government

Smith said the functions of government should be closely restricted. Since the natural laws of the market process could direct things so well, the government could only hurt things by interfering. People left alone would generate their maximum income (and wealth, well-being, and all that), so in sum, the *nation's* wealth would be maximized. Interference by the government could only reduce the nation's wealth and cut down on the economic well-being of the people.

Smith said the government should maintain law and order, protect the rights of private property, regulate the monetary system, and undertake the few necessary public projects—building harbors and highways and such things. But the government should *not* use the resources of the society for things the people would not want to spend their own money to pay for. The government should stay out of it and let the natural forces of the market direct and control the society's productive activities and resources.

Smith's Impact on Economic Thinking

Adam Smith's book was a great book at the time it was written. It is still a great book. It explained what was going on. To the businessman of the day, Smith gave a justification for selfish profit-seeking. To the poor he gave a promise of a better life through economic growth: Profits would be reinvested; more capital would be built; eventually there would be more income and a better life for everyone.

Smith showed how all the painful and seemingly heartless conditions could be justified by this larger picture—by long-run benefits for everybody. He showed how all this misery was really leading to something good in the future—something good in which all people would share. He explained that there was some *present purpose,* and some *ultimate relief* for all the hunger and misery in the world. Looked at from Smith's point of view, perhaps the miserable conditions of the early years of the industrial revolution weren't quite as hard to take.

Smith's explanation of the natural laws of economics—of how free market forces can control the economy and direct things into desirable directions—were destined to live on to the present time, and almost certainly beyond. But his optimistic conclusion about the outcome—about the *ultimate relief* for all the hunger and misery—about the long-run betterment of the economic welfare of the masses—this idea was soon to be challenged. By whom? By the next two great classical economists: the Reverend Thomas Robert Malthus and the self-made millionaire David Ricardo. But before we get into the ideas of Malthus and Ricardo, there's someone else who needs to be mentioned: Jeremy Bentham.

JEREMY BENTHAM

In the very same year the *Declaration of Independence* and the *Wealth of Nations* appeared, young Jeremy Bentham published his first book, too. But it wasn't until thirteen years later (in 1789) that his major work, *Principles of Morals and Legislation,* appeared. Bentham's book was not a book on political economy. It was not on the question of the wealth of the nation, but on "the welfare of the society—how to measure it and how to achieve it.

Bentham's book was a very different kind of economics book—but it was an economics book, just the same. It talked about how the wealth (the good things of the society) might be shared among the people for the greatest *total welfare*—for the "greatest good" the society could achieve.

Bentham's "Pleasure Measure"

Bentham's "Felicific Calculus" (his "pleasure-measure") was based on the idea that the greatest total welfare of the society would result from the greatest *sum total* of the welfare of all the individuals. If I might *lose* some "welfare"— and thereby you might *gain more* "welfare" than I lost, then there would be a net gain for the society. Get the idea? It's the idea of "the greatest good for the greatest number," of course.

What's so important about Bentham's contribution to classical economics? Just this: He explained the motives of the individual—the driving force which directs each individual's activities and behavior. Bentham said that each person is essentially a self-serving unit—that each individual is powered by the desire to do things which serve his own best interest—the desire to seek pleasant experiences and to avoid or escape from painful ones.

Bentham Analyzed the "Motive Force"

Remember how Adam Smith explained how the market system worked? How each person would act to serve his own interest, yet each would be guided "as though by an invisible hand" to serve the best interests of the society? How the only way one could get more of what *he* wanted would be by doing or making something somebody else wanted? Now do you see how Bentham's ideas fit in? Sure.

Smith talked about *how* individual self-interest is automatically directed toward improving the welfare of the society. Bentham dug into the self-interest question; he analyzed and offered new insights into the motive force— the engine which powered Smith's economic machine. He did that, and he did much more than that.

Bentham tried to explain man's behavior, and the things which influence the welfare of mankind in society. Some of his ideas can be found deeply imbedded in all of today's social sciences. Certainly his ideas influenced the next two classical economists we'll be talking about—two men who were greatly concerned about the record-breaking, historically unprecedented rate of population increase during the late 1700s and early 1800s. What two men? Malthus and Ricardo.

MALTHUS AND RICARDO

Thomas Malthus was only ten years old when *Wealth of Nations* was published. David Ricardo was only four. Obviously neither of them was very impressed with Adam Smith at the time! But as they grew up and observed the chaotic, miserable world in turmoil around them, they began to study, and to think. Then each in his own time decided that he had something to say. And each said it—to one another, and to the world.

Malthus and Ricardo Worked with the Natural Laws

Essentially both Malthus and Ricardo agreed with the natural laws of economics as presented in *Wealth of Nations.* They agreed that there was a sort of natural order in economic affairs and that the government should follow a policy of laissez-faire. Both Malthus and Ricardo published books called *Principles of Political Economy,* both about the same time (around 1820), not quite half a century after *Wealth of Nations* was published.

Both Malthus and Ricardo carried forward and added to what we call classical economics. Both writers helped to further explain the process of the market—how the free market forces can control and direct the economy. But both disagreed with Smith about the optimistic ultimate outcome of laissez-faire economics in the real world. Both said that *population expansion* would prevent the improvement of mankind's economic welfare.

Malthus said that for the poor, hard times were here to stay. He said that population would expand so rapidly that people always would be going hungry. The gains from increasing food production would be eaten up by the expanding population.

The Malthusian Law of Population

The population of Europe had more than doubled in the 1700s. In the 1790s Malthus wrote his *Essay on Population.* He said there was a tendency for the population to expand *more rapidly* than the food supply could expand. Therefore, most people's food consumption always would be held down to bare subsistence. Malthus admitted that people might voluntarily limit their reproductive urges and dodge this unpleasant outcome, but he didn't expect that they would.

This idea expressed by Malthus—that population expansion would keep the people poor and hungry—is called "the Malthusian Law of Population." It made a lot of sense at that time. It makes a lot of sense now.

In most of the less-developed nations of the world today, population growth is the greatest single obstacle to economic development and improved standards of living for the people. Whenever gains are made in production or in living conditions, population seems to expand and wipe out the gains.

Malthus dealt with more than just the population issue. He had more than that to say about economics. But he will always be best remembered for calling the attention of thinkers to the population problem—a problem which today is much more serious than it was then—a problem which some people now consider so serious as to threaten the continued existence of mankind on earth.

Ricardo Built a Theoretical Model of the Pure Market System

Ricardo was a brilliant economic theorist. He developed a theoretical model to show the intricate way in which the market process directs and controls the laissez-faire and competition economy. He emphasized the importance of the growth of capital through savings and investment. He could see that widespread poverty was contributing to growth. But, like Malthus, he was pessimistic about the future welfare of most of the people.

The Iron Law of Wages

Like Malthus, Ricardo agreed that the population would continue to expand and force wages to stay very low—at or near (sometimes below) the level of bare subsistence. Like Malthus, Ricardo agreed that if wages were *less* than subsistence, the population and the labor force would get smaller. People would die—more children would die of malnutrition and old or sick people would not survive as long. Young people would delay marriage and/or have fewer children. The work force would shrink. The shortage of workers would cause businessmen to overbid each other—to offer higher wages to try to hold on to their workers. Wages would be pushed upward to the subsistence level.

If wages ever got *above* the subsistence level, population would expand. People would marry earlier and have larger families. More children would be healthier and would survive and become workers. There would be more workers around than the businesses wanted to hire. The surplus workers would be trying to get jobs, underbidding each other. Workers would accept lower wages in order to get jobs, or to hold on to their jobs. Wages would be pushed down to subsistence again. Economic misery would be perpetuated. This bare subsistence theory of wages is sometimes called "the iron law of wages." No wonder economics in the early 1800s was called "the dismal science"!

High Food Costs Force Up Wages

Here are more of the results of Ricardo's model: Since wages must hover around the subsistence level, the higher the subsistence cost of living, the higher wages must be. If grain and other foods are cheap, the cost of subsistence will be low; the wages the manufacturer will have to pay will be low. The manufacturer's profits will be high. But suppose the cost of living is high. Then the subsistence level of wages will be high. The manufacturer's profits will be low.

With high living costs and therefore high wages and low profits, manufacturers will not have much money to invest in new capital. Economic growth will be stunted. Can you see why Ricardo fought against the high import tariffs on grain (the corn laws)? The corn laws increased the cost of living and therefore kept wages up. The higher wages reduced industry's profits and stunted economic growth! (Leave it to a sharp thinker like Ricardo to figure out something like that!)

The Profit Squeeze

Ricardo's analysis went much further. He went on to show that as the population expands, the cost of living will increase. As there are more and more people eating up the food supplies, more land areas will have to be cultivated. But the new land areas will be less and less fertile. Intelligent farmers will cultivate the best land first. No one will cultivate any *more* land (the poorer land) unless the price of grain goes high enough to pay the cost of growing the grain on the poorer land. Obviously! And it costs more (obviously) to grow grain on poor land. So the subsistence cost of living must go up. Then wages must go up. This squeezes profits. See what's happening?

Ricardo's Theory of Rent

Something else is happening, too. When the price of grain goes high enough to justify cultivating the *very poor* land, think of the high profits the owners will be making on the *very best* land! If you own a lot of good land and you have been making a pretty good rent from your wheat-growing tenants, think how much rent they will pay you so they can keep using your good land after the price of wheat goes up! This was Ricardo's "differential rent" theory.

Ricardo talked about the "marginal" land on which the farmer would just make enough to break even. This land could command no "rent." But any land which is more fertile than the marginal land would bring its owner a "surplus"—a *rent*. So as population expands, you see what is going to happen. Poorer and poorer lands will have to be cultivated. But higher prices will have to be paid for grain in order to get this to happen. Now, as the grain prices go up, the people who own the *fertile* land (and who were doing okay already) will find that they are beginning to make a lot more money.

The Landowners Receive Surplus Income

You can see that as the grain prices rise more and more, landowners will receive larger and larger *surplus incomes* from their fertile lands. This will put the landowners on easy street. The more the population expands, the more of the poorer lands must be farmed. So the higher must go the price of grain (and the cost of food, and the wages of labor), and the bigger will be the surplus incomes (rents) of the landlords. Can you see that rent is "price-determined" (determined by the demand for and the price of grain)? Sure. Oh to be a landlord!

What does Ricardo's model predict for the manufacturers—the ones who are making profits and investing in more and better capital and bringing about economic growth—adding more and more to the wealth of the nation? For them the prediction is not so good. As wages go up to pay for the high cost of food, profits are squeezed. As profits shrink, the boom slows down and stops. The industrial expansion gets choked off.

According to Ricardo, the economic deck was stacked in favor of the landowner and against everyone else. Ricardo concluded that by the very nature of the market system—by the natural laws which guided it—the landowners were bound to be big winners over the long run. The workers would be receiving just enough to live on, the capitalist-industrialists would be struggling to survive, and the wealthy landowners would be getting richer and richer as the rents for the land went higher and higher. (After Ricardo made his fortune in stocks, he invested in good land. He must have really believed in the real-world relevance of his theoretical model!)

The Long-Run Impact of Malthus and Ricardo

As history would have it, many of the predictions of both Malthus and Ricardo didn't come true exactly as they had expected. Both were making assumptions about the reasonable permanence of the world as they saw it, in their lifetimes. They didn't allow—they *couldn't* have allowed—for the explosive rate of change which at that time was already well underway. As it has turned out, population in the advanced countries has not expanded exactly as expected. Wages have risen *far* above subsistence. And technology and productivity in both agriculture and manufacturing have gone forward so much more rapidly than Malthus, Ricardo, or anyone else could have expected. It shows something about the perils of predicting. It was perilous then. It's probably just as perilous—maybe even more perilous—now.

Both Malthus and Ricardo made important contributions to the development of our present understanding of economics. The Malthusian Law of Population focused early on a problem which today is very real and very serious. Hunger in the poor nations and pollution in the cities are only two of the many present-day manifestations of rapid population expansion.

Ricardo's theoretical model identified and explained in detail many of the economic forces which previously had been understood only in general terms. His model helped us to see some of the "economic laws" at work in the world. Ricardo is considered by many to be the greatest economist of his time. Some might call him the greatest economist *of all time.* He was that good. His theoretical model of how the pure market process would work has had a profound influence on economic thought and policy from Ricardo's day to the present. And certainly Ricardo's influence on economic thought isn't all used up yet. It will go on, far into the future.

OTHER CLASSICAL ECONOMISTS

During the time of Malthus and Ricardo many others were thinking and writing about economic matters—about political economy. Jean Baptiste Say and James Mill were both about the same age as Malthus and Ricardo. J. B. Say was nine in 1776 when *Wealth of Nations* appeared. James Mill was three. Both these men published "Political Economy" books in the early 1800s. Both wrote in the classical tradition of Smith, Malthus, and Ricardo, explaining how the market process works—explaining the intricate workings of the market system. And there were several others— before, at the time of, and after Smith, Malthus, and Ricardo. But we just don't have time to talk about them all.

Say is best known for his "Law of Markets"—the idea that *supply* creates its own *demand.* The more a producer takes to the market (supply), the more he can get in trade (buy) and take home with him (demand). Say's law explains an important "natural balancing tendency" in the way markets operate. (As with other economic theories, Say's law doesn't always work out exactly right in the real world. But the tendency is there, and sometimes it's helpful to know about it.)

James Mill is not best known for his contributions to economic understanding, but for his contributions in history and political theory. But probably he is even better known as the father and teacher of a truly unique, great philosopher and economist of the nineteenth century—John Stuart Mill.

John Stuart Mill

John Stuart Mill was born in 1806. He was not yet fifteen years old when his father and his father's friends Malthus and Ricardo were coming out with their political economy books. But even at fifteen, he was ready for them. Very ready.

Ever since he had been about old enough to talk, John Stuart Mill had been studying under the demanding tutelage of his father. It is said that he was reading classical Greek at the age of three. (I don't know how well.) By the time he was thirteen he had finished his studies of Aristotle and Plato and the other philosophers who wrote in Greek and Latin. He had read profusely in English history and in other areas, had mastered calculus, had written history books and, among other things, was then studying the writings of Smith, Malthus, and Ricardo. All by the age of thirteen, would you believe!

Although he was writing on economics and various other subjects from the time of his teens, it was not until 1848 (when he was 42) that his *Principles of Political Economy* was published. This book became the leading text on economics for several decades. Much of John Stuart Mill's *Principles* was orthodox classical economics. It integrated much of what had been done by the various writers from Adam Smith on. It further clarified Ricardo's theoretical model of the pure market system. But it wasn't all orthodox. It challenged classical economics—specifically, the Ricardian model—on a very basic, fundamental point—on "the laws of distribution."

Mill Challenged Ricardo's Model

The Ricardian model described an economic system in which the pure market process was allowed virtually complete control over everything. People owning productive factors would produce. Those who produced could have something to consume. The iron law of wages kept the workingman's share low. Increasing rents kept the landlord's share high and rising. All this happened as the result of the natural market forces. To tamper with the results would be to interfere with the system. And that would only make matters worse. The poor people would stay poor, and that was that. John Stuart Mill challenged this conclusion.

Mill's point was this: It isn't necessary to let the natural market forces decide how much each person is going to get to eat. It is possible for the *society* to decide whether or not it wants some of its people to starve, while others (the landowners) are filthy rich and getting richer. He pointed out that the laws and customs of the society (that is, the political processes and the social processes—not just the market processes) can have a lot to say about how the output is directed.

At least to an extent, it's obvious that Mill was right on this point. In all modern societies the market forces are modified to take something away from the productive people and give a share to the nonproductive ones. But, of course, we have no way of knowing how much these "income redistributions" may have stunted growth, and contributed to low wages, high unemployment, and other undesirable effects. Economists wonder about things like that, but there's no sure way to find the answers to "what might have been."

Positive Economics and Normative Economics

Mill sort of straddled the line between what we call "positive economics" and "normative economics." *Positive economics* deals with the "laws" of economic behavior—that is, with general statements of fact: "If you don't pay a man to work for you he will not work for you." "If you offer a lot more money for corn than wheat, people will grow and sell you more corn than wheat." "If the fried chicken price doubles and the hamburger price goes down, people will buy less of the high-priced fried chicken and more of the low-priced hamburgers." These are statements of positive economics. Positive economics doesn't say it's

good or bad—it just tries to tell "what would happen if...."
It just tries to "tell it like it is."

Normative economics gets into the questions of how it ought to be—how to change things—how to make things better. Normative economics is what John Stuart Mill was talking about when he suggested that the society could distribute and share its products and resources among the people in the way they *wanted* to—in the way they thought *best.*

Ricardian economics is positive economics. Much of Mill's economics is also positive economics: "If you do so and so, then (if everything else stays the same) so and so will inevitably happen." But Mill also addressed some of the normative issues—the "value" issues—the issues of good or bad, right or wrong, better or worse, and of how to make the economic choices *better* for society. Yes, he sort of straddled the "positive-normative" fence. Perhaps that was the best thing for him to do—or perhaps not. Who knows? Certainly many (perhaps most) economists are doing it today.

What do you think? Should economists get involved in the issues of "what's best"? Or only "what is"? The "scientific tools of economic analysis" are tools of positive economics—of finding out and explaining "what is," and "what would happen if." When the economist gets into questions about how much income a family of four *should* have, and how high wages of unskilled workers *should* be, the scientific tools of economic analysis don't help at all. Still, when the economist talks about such things as guaranteed annual incomes, and minimum wages, he is at least *one* step ahead—he may be able to work up a pretty good answer to the question: "What would happen if the government decided to set up this program or that program?" or "What kind of program might we set up to achieve the objective?" Unless you know some positive economics, you don't know *what's* going to happen when the government (or somebody) changes something.

Economists are no better than anyone else at deciding what objectives we'd *like* to achieve. (No worse, mind you. But no better.) But economists are (or at least should be) better at working out feasible ways (and throwing out unfeasible ways) of getting to the objectives. Still, there are many economists who prefer to by-pass these issues entirely and spend their energies finding out more about the interrelationships among the variables in Ricardo-type models.

Which is the proper role for the economist? That question has been at issue for quite some time. It isn't likely to be solved today.

THE UTOPIAN SOCIALISTS

There were several philosophers about John Stuart Mill's time (and some before and some after) who didn't straddle the fence any more than Ricardo did. But they were on the *other* side of the fence—the normative side. We call these philosophers the "utopian socialists."

The Utopian Socialists Were Not Classical Economists

Most of the utopian socialists really didn't know much about the natural laws of positive economics. But they saw that the world looked like a miserable place for most people. They saw many rich and powerful people—industrialists, entrepreneurs—being very cruel to a lot of poor and hungry people. Men and women. Children too. The utopian socialists responded in various ways—but mostly unrealistically. The problem? They didn't understand some of the real-world limitations imposed by the natural laws of positive economics.

To be sure, some of the economic laws explained by the classical economists were only relevant in the *model* of the pure market system—not in the real world. Even today, economists are still finding out the disturbing fact that the results of our models are not always relevant in the real world. Sometimes we economists like to forget about the real world. It's so much neater to work with pure and predictable models than to get involved in the messy and unpredictable real world. But on the other hand, some of us enjoy the challenges of reality. And with our knowledge of economics we can approach the world with an awareness of and a very healthy respect for the economic facts of life— like the fact that "you can't have your cake and eat it too."

Most of the utopian socialists weren't bothered by the restricting influences of the laws of positive economics. But it's a fact of life that the economic laws which do hold true in the real world *are real.* Anyone who goes along trying to change things and ignoring these laws is inviting failure. Several of the utopian socialists did that. Let's talk about some of these interesting, dedicated, but not too realistic people—the utopian socialists.

There were several different, unique writers who can be grouped under the broad heading "utopian socialists." Who were they? What were their similarities? Their unifying characteristics? All of them were people who looked at the world, didn't like what they saw, and set about the task of trying to change it. Each had a different idea, a different approach. But generally, all were interested in trying to reorganize the society to get rid of the harshness and cruelty and to build in more love, friendship, sharing, and mutual assistance. Most of them worked for reforms to improve the conditions of the common people.

Saint-Simon and Fourier

In France there were two utopian socialists who were contemporaries of Malthus and Ricardo: Count Saint-Simon (pronounced SOHn-see-MOHn) and Charles Fourier (Foo-ree-A). Saint-Simon, an aristocrat himself, attacked as unjust the high incomes of the unproductive aristocrats. He founded a small religious sect—a sort of industrial religion. Fourier worked for the reorganization of people into communes, called "Phalanxes." Small groups of people would live in a big hotel—or those who preferred could live in a cluster of houses—and all would work for the good of the group.

Both of these French socialists had followers; people really did attend the Saint-Simonian churches, and Fourierist Phalanxes were actually set up in several places. Would you believe there were some forty of them in the United States in the early to mid-1800s? You may have heard of the Brook Farm community in Massachusetts (mid-1800s). Nathaniel Hawthorne joined it for awhile. Brook Farm was one of these Fourierist "utopian" communities. Two other well-known ones were the North American Phalanx at Red Bank, New Jersey, and the Wisconsin Phalanx.

We really don't need to go into much detail about the utopian socialists. The important thing is to be aware that while the classical economists were accepting certain things as given and trying to understand and explain what was going on, the utopian socialists were *refusing to accept* the givens. They didn't ask why, or where it was all going. They jumped right in and tried to change things. Each one approached the task in his own unique way.

One of these utopian socialists stands out, because he did accomplish some things. Not all that he wanted to accomplish—not by a long shot—but he did accomplish some things. The man was Robert Owen.

Robert Owen

The Englishman Robert Owen was one of the most interesting and versatile of the utopian socialists. Owen was in the same age group as the several classical economists we have been talking about. Owen, Malthus, Say, James Mill, Saint-Simon, and Fourier were all approaching or in their 30s at the beginning of the 1800s. They were all observing the same real-world conditions, but they certainly were interpreting them differently! Owen set out to improve the world.

Robert Owen started out as a poor boy and worked his way up in the textile industry. Eventually he owned and made a fortune operating a textile mill in Scotland. His mill and the local town were operated on policies which were, at that time, unbelievably humane. He was trying to prove that people would respond favorably to a benevolent environment. The profits of his mill seemed to prove his point; but no one else rushed to follow his example.

Like Fourier, Owen suggested that society be reorganized. He suggested that people set up "villages of cooperation." To prove that these villages would work, he sold his factory in Scotland, came to the United States, bought some land, and (in 1826) established a utopian community in Indiana.

Owen's new community was named New Harmony. Too bad it didn't live up to its name. Owen placed much trust in the people who came to join. As it turned out, it appears that there was too much trust and too little planning. In less than two years the community had fallen apart.

After the failure of New Harmony, Owen became a leader in the co-op and trade union movements in England. He never ceased to work, to write, to press political leaders, to urge for reform to help the common people. He worked hard at the task of improving the world, and he generated a sizeable following. His writings inspired several cooperative communities; he had a lasting impact on the labor and co-op movements in Britain. He is credited with coining the word "socialism."

The Effects of the Utopian Socialists

Both the utopian socialists and the classical economists were looking at and thinking about all the hardship and misery in the world around them. Some of the classical economists (Adam Smith and others) explained that all this hardship was *necessary* to serve the long run good of the society. Other classical economists said it was *inevitable*— that any attempt to ease the hardship and misery of the poor would only bring more suffering. The natural laws of economics said so. There could be no escape from these natural economic laws! But the utopian socialists refused to believe this. They would not accept and give in to the natural laws of economics. Really, most of them didn't even study these laws. They were too busy trying to change things.

The writings of the utopian socialists generally carried none of the precise and scientific analysis which is found in the writings of the classical economists. The utopian socialists weren't theoretical analysts. They were impatient activists. All of them had their followers, and all of them had some influence on the lives of some people. In the United States alone, more than 150 utopian communities were established, inspired by the philosophies and teachings of the utopian socialists. Most of the communities didn't last long—probably because they refused to recognize some basic laws of economics and some basic facts about the nature of human beings. But a few of the communities still exist (in modified form) even today.

The utopian socialists didn't help us much to understand the sweep of economic evolution, or to understand the natural economic forces at work in the world. But the lives of some people were influenced—perhaps improved. Some of the ideas and dreams of the utopians are still living, influencing the lives of some people, even today. These utopians cared a lot. And they fought hard. It's pleasant to think that some lasting good came from it all.

Now it's time for us to move on. We need to take a look at a very different "breed of cat"—people who were not nearly so mild and gentle, so optimistic and dreamy as the utopian socialists. These were angry, bitter, coldly logical people who were ready for the violent overthrow of the social, political, and economic systems which were permitting such hardships and misery to exist. Who? The communist revolutionaries. We'll talk about them and about some other people and some other things, in the next chapter.

3

RAPID CHANGES IN THEORY AND IN SOCIETY—THE EVOLUTION BECOMES EXPLOSIVE (1850s-1920s)

Marx Attacks Capitalism, Monopoly Power
Grows, Marshall Rebuilds Economics, and
The World Keeps on Changing

In 1848 the kind and gentle philosopher John Stuart Mill published his *Principles of Political Economy.* He raised a question about the Ricardian model and its natural economic laws of distribution. Remember? Well, in that same year there appeared a much different, most outspoken pamphlet which mounted a major attack on the market system. The pamphlet was *The Manifesto of the Communist Party.* Its principal author was a man you have already heard of: Karl Marx. In the *Communist Manifesto* Marx and his colleague Friedrich Engels called for revolution—for the workers to violently overthrow the governments in Europe, and take over the factories from the capitalists.

IN 1848, TIMES WERE BAD

Marx and Engels were looking at Europe in the mid-1800s. Conditions were bad. Very bad. There was hunger. Starvation. Popular revolts against the governments of several European countries seemed very likely. People were rioting in several cities—Paris, Brussels, Berlin, Prague, Vienna, and elsewhere. In France, King Louis Philippe was forced to resign. It was in this turmoil that Marx and Engels called for the workers of the world to unite, to forcibly overthrow their governments and take over the factories from the capitalists.

At that moment in history it looked very much like this Marxian revolution might really happen! But somehow things held together and ultimately began getting better for most people. Let's talk about this remarkable man who has had such a profound impact on the lives of all of us—this brilliant, angry "classical economist-revolutionary"—Karl Marx.

KARL MARX

Marx was in radical protest against "the system" throughout most of his life. He was born in Germany in 1818. That was when John Stuart Mill was twelve years old and the *Principles* books of both Malthus and Ricardo were about ready to appear. Before Marx was twenty-five years old he was already in trouble. He had studied philosophy (and had become an atheist). He went into journalism, began writing radical articles and got himself expelled from the German city of Cologne. Then he went to Paris, associated with socialists and other radicals, wrote more radical things and wound up getting kicked out of Paris. He went to Belgium, but after the *Communist Manifesto* appeared in 1848 (when Marx was thirty) he was exiled and went to England where he spent the remainder (the last thirty-five years) of his life.

Marx Lived in Poverty

During most of his life Marx was very poor—frequently hungry—often angry. During his thirty-five years in England (until his death in 1883) he studied the writings of the classical economists, the socialists, and other philosophers. And he thought, and wrote. In 1867, almost twenty years after the *Communist Manifesto,* he completed and published the first part, or "book" of *Das Kapital* (in English, *Capital*). The second part was not published until almost twenty years later—in 1885, two years after Marx's death. The third part did not appear until nine years later, in 1894. Parts two and three were published by Marx's long-time friend, colleague, and supporter, Friedrich Engels.

Marx Studied Ricardo, for a Purpose

During his years of study and thought (and poverty) in England, Marx became one of the great economists of the last century—and, really, of all time. But he was a revolutionary and an angry man long before he was a great economist. Marx studied the classical economists (especially Ricardo) long and hard, for a purpose. He was building a case to support his conviction—a conviction he had already stated (most forcefully!) in the *Communist Manifesto*.

Marx learned and then used the precise concepts, the "natural economic laws," of the Ricardian "market system" model to show that the model contained within itself "the seeds of its own destruction." Marx used the Ricardian model to prove that his (Marx's) already-stated convictions really were supported by natural economic laws—that the outcome was predictable. *Inevitable.*

It shouldn't surprise you that different people can look at the same real-world conditions and use the same economic concepts and yet arrive at very different conclusions about the ultimate outcome. Think back. Smith, Malthus, Ricardo, other classical economists all more or less agreed about the basic concepts—the "natural laws" of economics. They all agreed about laissez-faire and competition, and about the responsiveness of the factors of production to the demands of the society. Yet each came to a somewhat different conclusion about the future.

To Smith, everyone was going to share in the economic growth. To Malthus, the industrialists would do fine but the people would be poor. To Ricardo the landowners would ultimately be the really fat cats and their high surplus incomes (rents) would choke off economic growth. What

Marx did (in his *purely economic* writings) really was not so different from this. Smith, Malthus, and Ricardo all observed the same "natural forces" at work. But each came to a different (and, as history would have it, wrong) conclusion about the ultimate outcome. And so did Marx.

Marx Was A Classical Economist

Can you see that Marx the economist was really a classical economist, dealing with positive economics—even much more than, for example, John Stuart Mill? Mill challenged some of the "natural economic laws." Marx worked within them, and with them. Marx understood and used the principles of classical economics to support his conclusion about the ultimate collapse of the market-directed system—the collapse of the system which he had the honor of naming "capitalism." Now, let's talk about his big economics book.

DAS KAPITAL

Das Kapital is a most remarkable book. Just as *Wealth of Nations* at times shows us the thoughts and feelings of Smith the economist, and at other times Smith the anti-mercantilist; so *Das Kapital* reflects the several faces of its author. We see Marx the visionary, the revolutionist, the rejected philosopher, the hungry, angry, sometimes bitter man. But we also see Marx the meticulous, precise economist—the one who set out to build the airtight case showing the inevitable collapse and oblivion of this "most dastardly" economic system—capitalism.

In *Das Kapital,* Marx undertakes economic analysis with the precision of Ricardo. He uses the Ricardian laws to build his system and to explain the "inevitable sequence" of economic change—change that, to Marx, was predetermined within narrow limits by economic laws—by the natural economic forces at work in the society.

The Marxian theoretical system shows how the economic forces will lead to *inevitable revolution*—to the overthrow of capitalism. The careful, logical, precise explanation of how capitalism will lead itself to its own destruction is presented in detail in *Das Kapital.* The essence of the argument isn't difficult to understand. Here are some of the highlights.

Surplus Value

Marx agreed with Malthus and Ricardo about the iron law of wages—that wages will stay at about the subsistence level. But, said Marx, a worker doing a long day's work can produce *more* than enough for his subsistence. That is, the worker produces more "product value" than he receives in wages. He may work a fourteen-hour day (not particularly unusual in the mid-1800s) but he may produce enough "product value" to cover his wages in only eight hours. Everything he produces after that (the six extra hours'-worth of output) is surplus value. The surplus value goes to the capitalist. The capitalist exploits labor by keeping this surplus for himself—when it *really* belongs to the worker. (So said Marx.)

The Capitalist Exploits Labor

So Marx said that the capitalist gets profits from exploiting labor—from forcing the worker to work longer than he should work to earn his subsistence wage. Next, the capitalist invests this profit (surplus value) in more capital—factories, machines, equipment. Then, with all the new capital equipment, the expanding businesses need more labor. So they try to hire more people. This increases the demand for labor and pushes up the wage rate. So what does the capitalist do? He buys even more capital, to replace some of his high-wage workers. With more labor-saving capital, the capitalist can get by with less labor.

Ah, but the trap! To Marx, surplus value comes *only* from labor, and surplus value is the *only* source of profit for the industrialist. So, in the Marxian model, as the number of *workers* declines, *surplus value* falls. So profit falls. When profit falls, the capitalists will try to cut costs by introducing *even more* labor-saving equipment. But in the Marxian model this only makes matters worse. Obviously. The more the capitalists try to fight the fall in profits, the worse things get. So what's the answer?

Only a Few Capitalists Will Survive

Times get very bad. Depression. Some businesses go broke. When they do, other businesses buy up their capital for almost nothing. According to Marx, there will be one crisis after another until a very few, very large and powerful businessmen are in control of all the capital. They own just about all of the means of production. These wealthy people will have great monopoly power over all the others in the society. Also, they will have gained control of the government so they can make sure that the government will protect their *private property* rights.

Almost all of the people will be poor, hungry, wretched. The only way for this bad scene to be improved will be for the poor people—the "proletariat"—to overthrow the government. Then they can (and will) take back "their" capital from the wealthy "bourgeoisie" (BOOR-zhwa-zee). The capital was built out of the surplus value "stolen" from the workers (the proletarians), in the first place. It's rightfully theirs. So they take it back. Thus endeth capitalism. So says Marx.

What's going to happen after the overthrow of capitalism? Marx doesn't have much to say about that. At first things will be a little rough. The capitalist types will have to be gotten rid of. But after that, things are going to be much better. Ultimately a beautiful society will emerge. It will be built on the high productivity of the "reclaimed capital." All will share in the output. And without the selfish greed of the capitalists there will be enough for everyone to have all he wants. A beautiful world, right? The communist "true believers" are still waiting for it to happen just as Marx predicted. How utterly ridiculous. If Marx himself were alive today he would laugh (or be distressed) that anyone could be so stupid.

Instead of continuing down the harsh and bitter road which Marx expected, capitalism has been continually tempered more and more to soften the harshness—to lessen the socially unacceptable conditions of raw capitalism. And some progress has been made in limiting the monopoly power and controlling the market behavior of big firms. Certainly Marx never could have foreseen the extent of social justice that now exists in the world's "mixed economies of modified capitalism"!

Marx blamed the misery of the times on the capitalist system—not on the effects of a rapidly industrializing society caught in the early years of disruptive, explosive change. Marx was looking at the same world that Ricardo and John Stuart Mill were looking at. But because Marx looked at it in a different way he saw different things. The theories, ideas, concepts, and other preconceptions a person has in his mind when he looks at something often *determine* what he will see. This was as true of Marx (and of Ricardo and Mill) as it is of you and me.

The Lasting Impact of Karl Marx

Marx really gave the economists some things to think about. He made some contributions to our understanding of how the market system functions. But, of course, his predictions did not come true.

Did Marx have an impact on economics? On the world? You know the answer to that. It would be difficult to find anyone who has had more impact. He inspired and gave a rationale, a justification, for the revolutions in the Soviet Union, China, Cuba, and elsewhere. His writings have been carried forward by several neo-Marxist philosophers and revolutionaries—Lenin and others in the Soviet Union, Mao Tse-tung and others in China, Castro and others in Cuba, and others who can be found in most nations throughout the world.

It was Marx who first gave these people a logical position on which to stand—a way to justify revolting and taking over the private property of the capitalists. There is no question that Marx has left an indelible mark on the world.

NEW PROBLEMS EMERGE: THE PROBLEM OF MONOPOLY

During the late 1800s and early 1900s, two kinds of problems were emerging. One was the problem of increasing monopoly power. The other was the problem of recurrent financial panics and depressions. According to the theories of the market system, neither of these problems was supposed to happen. But both of them *were* happening.

During the decades when Marx was studying and writing, the rate of economic change seemed to become more and more explosive and more violent—rapidly expanding production of coal, oil, and steel; rapidly expanding use of steam power, railroads, and ships; the growth of industrial centers—truly phenomenal! And trade within and between nations was growing rapidly. The rate of change surpassed anything the world had ever known.

A Few People Got Very Wealthy

While the industrializing nations were growing explosively, some businesses were doing the same thing. They were developing and using new technology, becoming more efficient, making big profits—and building more capital to make more profits. By the end of the 1800s, the names of such Americans as John D. Rockefeller, Andrew Carnegie, and J. P. Morgan were household words. These were some of the powerful industrial and financial giants who were building mammoth business organizations, with monopoly positions in oil, steel, railroads, and other industries. Some people were becoming concerned about all this bigness—all this concentration of economic power in the hands of a few individuals and families.

Throughout the 1800s in the United States, England, and Western Europe, wages remained low. Profits were often very high. The rate of industrial invention, innovation, and growth was phenomenal. Output continually expanded. Some of the increased output consisted of consumer goods for the rapidly growing population. But much of the output was made up of new industrial machinery, basic materials, steel rails, new factories, and so on—the essential inputs for economic growth.

Increasing Concern about Growing Monopolies

By the late 1800s, more and more people began to be concerned about the rapid growth and mammoth size of some of the industrial corporations. More than a hundred years had passed since Adam Smith's *Wealth of Nations* had appeared, and more than half a century had elapsed since Ricardo developed his theoretical model of the pure market system. The laissez-faire idea was strongly embedded in the philosophy of the Western world. Still, people were beginning to worry about the growing power of big businesses.

It was well known that for laissez-faire to work, effective competition was required. Only competition prevents big businesses from exploiting their workers, the consumers, the resource suppliers, the landowners, and everyone else. The writings of Marx helped to emphasize the need for concern about big business—about industrial monopolies. Various groups began to call for limitations on the monopoly powers of businesses.

The Antitrust Laws

In 1887 the United States Congress passed the Interstate Commerce Act, regulating the railroads. The Act established the Interstate Commerce Commission to set rail rates and to see to it that the railroads provided adequate service to their customers. This was a start. Three years later the basic antitrust law in the United States was passed—the Sherman Antitrust Act.

The Sherman Antitrust Act (1890). The Sherman Act made it illegal for businesses to put their assets into a "trust," or to otherwise pool their assets to eliminate competition among themselves. This Act made it illegal for businesses to reduce competition either (a) by getting together with their competitors, or (b) by destroying their competitors. Businesses were using both these tactics to gain monopoly power to restrict supply (that is, restrain trade) and push up and hold up the price.

The phrase "restraint of trade," which means businesses stop selling in competition with each other, was used in the Sherman Antitrust Act because there had to be some constitutional justification for the federal government to pass laws regulating businesses. The U.S. Constitution does not give this specific power to the federal government. But the Congress found the constitutional justification they needed in Article I, Section 8. This section grants to the federal government the specific power to regulate interstate commerce (interstate trade). So the Congress just made it illegal for businesses to combine, or to conspire to restrain interstate trade. That made the Sherman Act constitutional.

The Clayton and FTC Acts (1914). The Sherman Antitrust Act was not noted for its success. In the 1890s and on up to the beginning of World War I, big businesses in the United States (and throughout Britain and Western Europe as well) continued to combine and expand. In 1911, two big monopolies in the United States—Rockefeller's Standard Oil Company and the Duke brothers' American Tobacco Company—were broken into smaller units by order of the Supreme Court. But other big businesses continued to grow. In 1914, the U.S. Congress passed two more antitrust laws—the Clayton Act and the Federal Trade Commission (FTC) Act—to try to further restrict the powers of businesses to get together to eliminate competition and/or to deceive their customers or engage in other socially undesirable activities.

How Bad Is the Monopoly Problem?

Neither the Sherman Act nor the Clayton Act nor the FTC Act was really effective in maintaining a high level of competition in American industry. In most of the other countries of the Western world, even less action was taken to curb the growing monopoly power of the industrial giants. There is no question that considerable monopoly power existed, and still exists, in the United States and throughout the industrialized world. How bad is this? How much does it interfere with the proper working of the market process? No one really knows.

Everyone knows that without some kind of effective competition, laissez-faire is a license to steal. On the other hand, everyone knows that we aren't going to have so many sellers and buyers in every market that no one has *any* monopoly power at all! Of course not. In today's world, pure competitive markets for everything are completely out of the question. Arguments about whether or not a real-world economy made up entirely of such markets would result in efficiency or inefficiency, stability or instability, growth or stagnation, or whatever—are just no help at all in getting the answers to the questions: "How bad is the monopoly problem today?" and "What should be done?"

The Basic Dilemma of "Bigness"

The monopoly issue presents the policy makers with a dilemma: We want all the advantages of bigness: stability, financial security for workers and for local communities, social responsibility, outstanding management, research and development and innovation—all that and more. But at the same time we don't want to let anyone escape from "effective competition." We don't want anyone to get a license to steal. We would like to have our cake and eat it too—to have all the advantages of bigness and of smallness at the same time. But of course we can't.

Many economists say that for the most part some kind of effective competition does exist in the modern world of "mixed socio-capitalism." Various explanations have been offered as to how this effective competition works. Other economists (and noneconomists, too) charge that big businesses have *too much* power and that they should be either (a) broken up into smaller, more competitive units, or (b) more closely regulated by the government, or (c) taken over by the government. It is not likely that these conflicting views are going to be resolved soon. Now it's time to get back to our story. (You'll see more about the monopoly problem in Chapter 6.)

THE "NEW WORLD" OF THE EARLY 1900s

Judged by almost any measure you can choose, the "developed" world of 1900 was truly a different world from that of 1800. Never before in history had there been anything like it. In one short century (less, really) the total number of human beings in the developed countries more than doubled. In the most rapidly growing places the population expansion was as high as tenfold or more. The techniques of production were almost completely different. The total outputs of industrial and agricultural products were many times as great. The rate of change had become explosive!

The Early 1900s: Heyday of Capitalism

Some economists like to say that it was during the first decade or so of our century—during the period from 1900 to about the beginning of World War I—that old-style Western capitalism reached its peak of glory. Outputs had expanded greatly. Businesses had very few restrictions and paid very little in taxes. Economic growth was rapid.

The trading nations were on "the international gold standard." This meant that international trade could move easily. Since all the countries used gold as their basic money, anyone could use gold (if necessary) to buy things from foreigners. World trade was carried on with very little restriction. The trading nations were prospering. The industrial and commercial enterprises were profiting and growing. Everyone was enjoying economic expansion, and everyone seemed to be benefiting.

World War I brought an end to all this. It marked the end of an era. Many people have tried to bring back the old era. Some are still trying. But it has never and will never work that way again. You who are aware of the explosive change now in command of our world could have guessed that. Measured by the extent of change, the years before World War I (in historical time) were many centuries ago! If some people want to be nostalgic about it, okay. But bring it back? No chance.

It's natural to want things to settle down and stabilize someplace. When so many things are changing so fast all the time, we all get confused—it's hard to know what's going on! But that seems to be the nature of our moment in history. And if that's the way it is, best we recognize it and somehow learn to live with it.

The Problem of Depressions

Throughout the late 1800s and the early 1900s, a series of financial panics and depressions occurred. Periods of depression have been noted as far back as the 1700s. Malthus recognized the possibility that "general gluts" (overproduction) might sometimes present a problem. Ricardo and others considered depression conditions to be temporary, short-run, and automatically self-correcting. Nothing to worry about. If there was a surplus of anything—labor, or products—the price of whatever was in surplus soon would go down. Then, at the lower prices, the surpluses would be bought up, and presto! No more surpluses! It was as simple as that. Depression just wasn't a matter of much concern to the classical economists.

So during the late 1800s and early 1900s while the problems of monopoly power and repeated depressions were bombarding the world, what were the economists doing? Addressing themselves to these issues? Generally, no. Economists continued to argue with each other and to refine their models of how the pure market process works. It was not to be until the 1930s that major breakthroughs were made by the economics profession in the analysis and understanding of these two problems—the problem of depression and the problem of monopoly power.

NEOCLASSICAL ECONOMICS

During the time the last parts of *Das Kapital* were appearing (the late 1800s) the neoclassical (new classical) school of economics was adding its modifications and refinements to the Ricardian model. Also, a number of schools of economic thought were developing. Each one was aiming off more or less in its own direction.

Disillusionment with Economics in the Late 1800s

During the late 1800s there was a good bit of confusion and some disillusionment about economics. Economists were busy disagreeing among themselves, and the theories of economics didn't seem to be much good in explaining the urgent problems of the real world.

Three major schools of thought arose: the German historical school, the Austrian marginalist school, and the neoclassical school. It was an Englishman of the neoclassical school—the Cambridge University economics professor Alfred Marshall—who "rebuilt" economics. By drawing on the works of the classical economists and integrating the marginal concept from his contemporaries of the Austrian school, Marshall pulled it all back together again.

Neoclassical economics pushed aside and/or modified several · of the natural economic laws of the classical economists. Something had to be done about the idea of the inescapable inevitability of the laws—of the Malthusian Law of Population, of the iron law of wages, of the labor theory of value (Marx's law that value comes only from labor), and several others. In the industrializing world of the *earlier* 1800s these "laws" seemed to fit real life, to be perpetual, immutable. But in the industrialized and rapidly changing world of the *late* 1800s, anyone could see that these laws simply weren't holding true. No wonder the esteem of economics (and economists) was slipping!

It was becoming obvious that some of the basic ideas and concepts of economics needed changing. And the *marginal concept* needed to be brought in. The neoclassical economists took care of these problems for us. But that isn't all they did. They sharpened the theoretical model of the pure market system. And they used the model to show how free people and free markets (laissez-faire and perfect competition) would bring maximum welfare for the whole society. Let's talk about Alfred Marshall and his reconstruction of economics.

Alfred Marshall's Principles of Economics

Marshall's *Principles of Economics*—"the new Bible," the complete integration, synthesis, and explanation of neoclassical economics—came out in 1890, the same year the U.S. Congress passed the Sherman Antitrust Act. Marshall's *Principles* was the latest word on neoclassical economics. It explains the workings of a laissez-faire, competitive market system. It shows very precisely and in detail how the total welfare of the society would be maximized in a "theoretical model economic system" of laissez-faire and perfect competition—that is, in a model economy directed entirely by the market process.

Marshall's *Principles* explained—and used supply and demand graphs to show precisely—how the market process directs the economy in response to the wishes of the society. Marshall's *Principles* lets you actually *see* (graphically) how the price mechanism directs the resources of the society into the best places—how it gets all the resources to do the best things.

Marshall's *Principles* went through eight editions. It was *the* economics book throughout the world for some thirty years. It was widely used up to and beyond the time of Marshall's death, in 1924. It is still a good book to study, to see how the theoretical model of the pure market system works—how it brings maximum welfare to the people of a society.

Marshall Had Many Contemporaries

There were many other neoclassical economists, and many challengers, in the late 1800s and early 1900s. In England, France, Germany, Austria, Italy, Scandinavia, and other countries, there were scholars, teachers, businessmen, politicians, and others, all working to develop new economic ideas and to influence economic thinking. Some made important contributions to our understanding of economic theory—of the cause-and-effect interrelationships in the economy.

LEON WALRAS AND GENERAL EQUILIBRIUM THEORY

One who made a very important contribution was Leon Walras (val-RAHs). You probably don't know it, but *neoclassical* economic theory rests on what we call *"partial equilibrium analysis."* This means we assume that "everything else stays the same," then we try to see what would happen if there was too much corn and not enough tomatoes. You know what would happen. The price of corn would go down and the price of tomatoes would go up. People would start growing more tomatoes and less corn. Pretty soon the problem would be solved. This is partial equilibrium analysis.

Partial equilibrium analysis doesn't tell us anything about what happens to the price of Iowa corn land, the demand for tomato pickers, the number of pickup trucks running from Ames to Waterloo, the demand for steel to make farm tractors, or any of the other hundreds of things which, in fact, will *not* "stay the same." Suppose there was some kind of theoretical system which could take into account all these simultaneous changes and show how it all works out. That would be a *"general* equilibrium analysis." Now can you guess what Walras did? Of course: He developed a *general* equilibrium analysis.

General equilibrium analysis is not any more difficult to understand than anything else, but it takes time. And we just don't have the time. All you need to remember is that Walras built a theoretical model which tied the whole economic system together. It shows how any change in one thing will cause changes in other things and how all these changes will work themselves out throughout the entire system. And after all the changes have worked themselves out, the economy will be in a new general equilibrium.

Walras used a system of mathematical equations as his model of the total economic system. Each equation represented one part of the economy, and all the equations were tied in with each other so that any change in one caused changes in all the others. Walras enabled economists to see the total picture. He showed that the theoretical model of a pure market economy really does all fit together, that it really is a self-contained, "mutually determined system"— that everything really does work out right. For this, Walras deserves to be listed among the greatest economists of all time. Some even suggest that his name ought to be at the top of the list.

SOME DISSENTERS: HENRY GEORGE AND THORSTEIN VEBLEN

There were many other economists who did important things. But it wouldn't do you any good to read and memorize a long list of strange-sounding names, with a list of major contributions to go with each. You would forget all that in a few weeks (or a few hours), anyway. I will mention only two more, both dissenters: Henry George and Thorstein Veblen.

Henry George and the Single Tax

In the late 1800s Henry George wrote his very popular book *Progress and Poverty*. The one point of his book was that the economic system should not permit lucky landowners to get wealthy just because they happened to own some land in a good place—like Manhattan Island or some other place where a city is going to grow up, or where a railroad is going to come through, or where oil is going to be discovered, or where something else lucky is going to happen. He said these landowners do nothing to deserve their wealth. Their wealth is unplanned, unnecessary, and *undeserved*—a rip-off.

Henry George suggested that the money landowners get from this kind of undeserved good luck should be taxed away. This land tax should be the "single tax"—the only tax necessary. The land tax revenues would be great enough so that no other taxes would need to be levied. Henry George had an interesting thesis and a large number of followers. He gave all of us something to think about.

Thorstein Veblen and Conspicuous Consumption

Thorstein Veblen was an unusual and interesting person and a brilliant and challenging economist. He was a professor at the University of Chicago in 1899 when he wrote his very popular book *The Theory of the Leisure Class.* Veblen criticized the whole approach of materialistic society—the "keeping up with the Joneses" hangup which he saw in American life.

One of Veblen's best known phrases is "conspicuous consumption." It's the idea that people buy and use up things unnecessarily, just to show off. Veblen thought that conspicuous consumption was inherent in the market system, and that it results in a great waste of resources.

In the early 1900s, Veblen wrote several more books. All of them carried forward his initial thesis—that the market economy as it works in the real world is aimed off in the wrong direction. It's wasteful, and too much influenced by rich people with vested interests. He predicted continuing, rapid technological and sociological changes and readjustments in the society. His impact on economics and on economists was (and is) great. Many of today's economic policies and programs—for consumer protection, income redistribution, and others—have deep roots somewhere in Veblen's theories and philosophy.

OLD-STYLE CAPITALISM'S LAST BURST OF GLORY: THE 1920s

To be sure, capitalism had its dissenters. There were many in addition to Henry George and Thorstein Veblen. The neo-Marxists continued to be active—to be sure! The Bolshevik (communist) Revolution occurred in Russia in 1917. But for the most part the Western world was little touched by the dissenters.

The Social Ethic Supports Capitalism

Capitalism was strong, productive, growing, and clearly justified by its religious and social ethics. By now, everyone had somehow learned the Protestant Ethic: "God helps those who help themselves." "The idle mind is the Devil's workshop." *"Work* for the Night is Coming." Everyone had learned to believe that if a man is poor, then he should be poor. He's poor because that's what he deserves. He hasn't worked hard enough to deserve anything better.

You can tell a person's worth by what he owns. Poverty is a sign of worthlessness. Poor people are no good. But rich people are respectable. A wealthy person is good and worthy and should be looked up to. Such were the generally accepted values of capitalism.

In the United States in the 1920s, economic expansion continued. The conditions of most of the people seemed to be improving, and (with the exception of some problems in agriculture) economic harmony and a happy life for most people seemed to have arrived. Of course, nothing was said about the "invisible members" of the society. But it is only in more recent years that people seem to have taken much notice of the minority people—the very poor, the dispossessed, the underprivileged, the discriminated against, or the incapable and unsupported ones.

Prosperity, Then Depression

By the late 1920s, the American economy was heralded as being on a high plateau. People talked about how difficult it would be to think of anything better. The economics of Britain and all of Western Europe had largely overcome the destructive effects of World War I. It seemed for a moment that economic conditions in the world were going to be all right again—that the golden age of the early 1900s was about to remanifest itself. But as you know, this was not our destiny. Instead, the whole economic structure was about to fall apart. A sudden, powerful, bewildering change was coming. The American—and world—economy was about to move into the Great Depression of the 1930s.

Probably you've already heard a lot about the Great Depression. What a confusing, bewildering time of social, economic, and political turmoil that was! We'll get into that (and more) in the next chapter. But before we go on we need to take one more brief glance back into history—one more look at this explosive change we're all caught up in.

THE FRUSTRATIONS OF RAPID CHANGE

It's difficult for you to realize how much change actually has occurred in your lifetime. Throughout almost all of the history of mankind it would have taken several centuries to accumulate the total amount of change which has occurred since you were born—or since you were in fourth grade, even! It's no wonder that man's understanding of economic happenings has had some difficulty keeping up with the changing times.

Here's something to think about:

Back in history, how long do you expect it would actually have taken to bring about as much change as you have seen in your lifetime? Just think about the degree of sameness—the very, very slow rate of change—over the twenty-five centuries from Babylonia to ancient Rome and Greece (about 3000 to 500 BC); and then during the five centuries of the Greek and Roman city-states (about 500 BC to 1); and then during the five centuries of the Roman Empire (about AD 1 to AD 500); and then during the next ten centuries of the Middle Ages, up to the discovery of America (about 500 to 1500); and then even in the three more "mercantilist" centuries which led up to the beginning of the United States (about 1500 to 1800).

The pace of change was quickening some during the mercantilist period. But throughout most of history, just think how very long it took for even the smallest change to take place! In any one *century* there might not be enough change—economic or any other kind—to notice.

Then, approaching the 1800s, the Industrial Revolution somehow got started. During the 1800s it burst forth, breaking everything loose, disrupting and changing everything. We have been blasted off on a journey of increasing speed, away from yesterday. And toward what? Toward an unknown—an unknowable—tomorrow.

As you read in the chapters coming up about all the changes happening in our own century, stop to think once in a while about how *unbelievably fast* it's all happening. Perhaps that will help you to understand this brand new ball game in which humanity suddenly finds itself forced to play. Perhaps it will help you to be more tolerant of your parents, your government leaders, your college administrators, your professors—and perhaps yourself—when you find that the game doesn't seem to be going as you think it should.

4

THE GREAT DEPRESSION
AND KEYNESIAN ECONOMICS
(1930s-1940s)

Neoclassical Economics Couldn't Explain
The Depression, So Some New
Approaches Were Developed

In October of 1929 the bubble burst. The decade of the 1920s had been one of growth, prosperity, good times, high employment, happy days for almost everyone. The total real value of the nation's output (value of goods and services produced) had increased from about $73 billion in 1920, to more than $100 billion in 1929—a total increase of more than forty percent.

Population was expanding, of course. More people were sharing this larger output. But even so, output *per person* increased by about 25 percent over this decade. When Herbert Hoover accepted the nomination of the Republican Party in 1928 he said: "We shall soon with the help of God be in sight of the day when poverty will be banished from this nation." But as you very well know, things didn't turn out that way.

The Stock Market Boom

Throughout the decade of the '20s, while employment and output were increasing, prices of stocks on the stock markets were going up faster and faster and faster. Throughout the first half of the decade, stock prices increased only moderately. Then the speedup began. A person holding an average group of stocks in 1925 would have seen their value increase by about 50 percent before the end of 1926—a 50 percent increase in about one year? Right! And the same thing happened again in 1927.

Ten thousand dollars invested in "an average group" of stocks in 1925 would be worth about $20,000 before the end of 1927. Before another year had passed, that $20,000 would just about double again—to about $40,000 before the end of 1928. And by August of 1929? Would you believe it doubled again? And more? That $10,000 investment in stocks in 1925 would very likely have reached a value of $100,000 before the crash came in October 1929.

Here's another thing: A person could have bought that $10,000 worth of stocks for as little as *10 percent down.* So for an actual cash investment of $1,000 in 1925, the "average person" would have wound up with $100,000 in 1929. Is it any wonder that everyone was "playing the stock market"?

The Stock Market Collapsed

By 1929 the ever-growing demand for stocks had pushed stock prices up far beyond the *real* values of the assets which the stocks represented. Many people knew they were holding overvalued stocks. But as long as stock prices kept on going up, why sell? Then, in the fall of 1929, some investors began to sell, to get their cash. This selling pushed down stock prices and caused others to lose confidence. There was more and more selling until finally, on October 29, the market collapsed. Everyone was trying to sell but no one was buying. Stock prices tumbled.

Economic Conditions Got Worse and Worse

For the next three years stock prices kept falling. If a person had owned $100,000 in General Electric stock in 1929, by 1932 his "fortune" would be worth about $3000.

As stock prices fell, month after month, businesses continued to fail. Unemployment increased. Banks continued to close. Economic collapse continued to visit one company after another, one place after another, one family after another. There seemed to be no end to the downtrend.

THE GREAT DEPRESSION

Each year it seemed that conditions were so bad they couldn't get any worse. But the next year *was* worse. Some people were actually starving in the cities. Food—grain, potatoes, livestock—was going to waste on the farms. Crops were rotting in the fields. Sometimes food prices were so low in the cities that it didn't even pay to ship the goods to market. The farmer couldn't get enough for his potatoes to pay the freight bill!

People in the cities were hungry, all right. But they didn't have any money. They couldn't buy the potatoes which were already there in the city, getting old in the grocers' storerooms. The economic system just wasn't working.

During this period many people in the United States joined the Communist Party. Veterans of World War I marched on Washington demanding that the government do something to help. The people didn't understand what was going on, but they knew they were hungry. Surely *any kind* of economic system must be better than this! An economic system that lets people starve while goods go to waste is obviously not doing a very good job. A person doesn't have to study economics to figure that out!

The Market System Wasn't Working

The market system is supposed to work by getting people to produce things for other people. That's the way each person gets the things he wants for himself. It's all supposed to work out very neatly. But during the depression the markets weren't working, so the system wasn't working. The system just sort of broke down!

The people in the cities were wondering how they could get some potatoes to feed their families. The farmers were wondering how they could sell their potatoes so they could get some money to pay their debts and to keep going. But the city people had no jobs and no money so they couldn't buy, so the farmers couldn't sell. When nobody's buying, then nobody's selling. The market system just isn't working.

The potatoes rotted in the fields. The city families went hungry. What had gone wrong with the world? What was causing all these bad times? How do we fix things? Nobody seemed to know.

No One Knew What Was Happening, or What to Do

The nation's leaders asked their economist-advisors what was happening, and why, and when things were going to start getting better. But the economists didn't know. This was some kind of new situation. Neither the classical nor the neoclassical nor any of the other theories of economics were of much help in explaining how such serious and prolonged depressed conditions could exist—or what (if anything) might be done to get things going again.

It was easy to see that the model of the pure market system wasn't much good for explaining what was going on. This was some kind of new problem—a brand new ball game—a game the economists hadn't yet learned to play.

Conditions Were Really Bad

The U.S. economy and the economies of the other free nations of the world kept getting worse and worse throughout the early 1930s. Then in 1933 things leveled off at a very low level. There was serious depression—U.S. and worldwide. There were some improvements over the next five or six years, but not much: The U.S. economy didn't really recover.

In 1933 the total output of the U.S. economy was only about one-half the size of the 1929 output. More than 25 percent of the people who wanted to work couldn't find jobs, so they (and their families) had no incomes. The families of most farmers and fishermen were living in serious poverty. Some of the lucky ones who had jobs were getting paid *less than* (would you believe?) $10 a month. In many parts of the country a wage of $20 a month was considered very good. People were begging for jobs—for *any* way to make money, at *any* wage.

Between 1929 and 1933, some 85,000 businesses failed. One bank out of every five went out of business. Some *nine million people* lost their savings accounts as the banks collapsed. On March 4, 1933, the U.S. government ordered all the banks in the country to be closed—that was to keep *all* the banks from failing under the increased assault of panic-stricken people withdrawing their deposits, demanding cash.

Things really were miserable. There were millions of hungry, desperate people. It's no wonder that some committed suicide—and that many joined the Communist Party. And it's no wonder that some committed crimes just to be sent to jail—where they could get shelter and food. I don't suppose freedom or liberty has very great appeal to one who is freezing or starving to death. Many Americans found that out in the 1930s.

The Depression Went On for Many Years

It's hard to believe how long this Great Depression lasted. It never got any worse than it was in March 1933, but as the years passed it didn't get much better. The government was trying out all kinds of programs. We'll talk about those in a minute. But the economy just didn't seem to respond very well.

Things got somewhat better in '35 and '36, but then in '37 and '38 there was another sharp drop. Unemployment all this time had been more than 15 percent of the labor force. In 1938, it was almost 20 percent of the labor force. Some ten million people were out of work. Also, in 1938 big surpluses began piling up on the farms again. Farm prices fell again.

Government Military Spending Overcame the Depression

It wasn't until 1939, when the government began to increase spending for military production, that total recovery began. By 1944 there was virtually no unemployment. The value of the nation's output was double that of 1929. Half the total output was being produced in response to the huge military spending program of the government. The government alone spent as much in 1944 as *total spending in the economy* had been in 1929 (about $100 billion).

See what happened when the government began its unlimited spending for World War II? How quickly the economic system began running full speed again! No more depression. No more unemployment. No more idle factories or unused surpluses of farm products or labor or anything else. A miraculous recovery! This experience taught us one thing: If the government is willing to spend enough money to employ enough people and buy enough output, it certainly can overcome a depression.

Did the government wait for World War II before it tried to do anything about the depression? Of course not. Lots of things were tried. Some helped, some didn't. Let's look back and see what the government was doing, and what new ideas the economists were coming up with during this long, miserable, bewildering decade of the 1930s.

THE NEW DEAL: BASIC CHANGES IN THE AMERICAN ECONOMIC SYSTEM

With things so bad and getting worse following the stock market crash in October 1929, people were urging the government to do something. Many voices clamored for government action. The clamor came from businesses large and small, from state and local governments, from welfare agencies and private charities, from religious organizations, from groups of irate citizens, from just about everybody. The veterans of World War I marched on Washington demanding relief. Everyone was confused. No one understood the situation. No one knew what to do. When Franklin D. Roosevelt was inaugurated on March 3, 1933, he promised to do something. He promised a "New Deal." He promised *action*. A real flurry of action is what he delivered. When he was all through, the American economic system was a *different* economic system than it had been before. A *better* system? Perhaps. Some people disagree on this. But everyone agrees that it was different.

What Was the New Deal?

What was meant by the "New Deal"? You can answer that question in many different ways. One way would be to list the fifteen or so major pieces of legislation which were pushed through Congress during the first 100 days after Roosevelt took office, and to describe the impact of these important federal acts on how the American economic system functions.

Another way to answer the question "What was the New Deal?" is to say that it was an idea, a concept, a vision of major change in the American economic system—a change away from the philosophies and policies of laissez-faire. The idea was that we were going to "reshuffle the cards and deal them out again"—to give the people with "bad hands" a chance to do better—that is, a "new deal."

This New Deal means that we will give the farmers some help, and some economic power to protect themselves from economic adversity. We will let workers join unions and bargain with (and if they wish, strike against) their employers. We will establish a social security program so that the welfare of each individual will not be just his own responsibility, but a responsibility shared by all members of the society.

The New Deal tried to do something specific, something direct to help those who were in difficulty—and that included farmers, workers, businesses, young people, old people, city people, country people: just about everyone. The government started programs to employ people, and to buy up the surplus food and give it to people.

Increasing the Economic Role of Government

Ideas about the proper role of government were changing fast. The New Deal idea was that wages and farm prices need to be kept high enough to support people adequately; that people have a right to live in decent housing—and that the government has a responsibility to *do something* to bring about these results. The New Deal also included the ideas that the banks and stock markets and other financial businesses should be watched over and regulated by the government to be sure the interests of the people are protected; and that the government should watch over and regulate employment practices, should prohibit child labor, should set limits on the length of the work week, and should require that higher wages be paid for overtime work. And there were many other changes to the economic system—all away from laissez-faire toward more influence and control by government in the economy.

A New Philosophy: Challenge to Laissez-Faire

Perhaps we could summarize the philosophy of the New Deal this way: "It is the responsibility of the government to be concerned about the operation of the economic system, and about the material welfare of the people. The government has a responsibility to keep the system running properly, to oversee all of the activities within the economic system which might adversely affect the lives and conditions of the people of the society, and to see to it that everyone has an opportunity to share in the high level of well-being which this 'modern economic system' can produce. Even those people who are unproductive—because of health or age or unemployment or some other misfortune—should still get a share of the output. The government should take some income from the productive people and give it to the unproductive ones."

What a basic change this New Deal was! The American economic system *before* the New Deal was quite a different system from the American economic system *after* the New Deal. *Quite* a different system! It's no wonder that many people—especially those who had been enjoying most of the benefits of the pre-New Deal system—were violently opposed to President Franklin D. Roosevelt's New Deal.

But in 1933 and the years following, almost everyone was feeling the squeeze of the depression. Most of the people were disillusioned, confused, bewildered. The depression had been dragging on, getting worse and worse each year. People who in 1929 would have considered the New Deal subversive and un-American (or maybe even a Communist take-over!), in 1933 were ready to try anything. By then it was obvious to most people that sitting around waiting for the natural forces of the laissez-faire market system to solve the problem just wasn't the answer.

The real world wasn't behaving the way the neoclassical model said it should. The model just didn't fit the reality of the 1930s. So what happened? What *always* happens when the theoretical explanations don't offer workable solutions to the real world's economic problems? Pragmatism takes over? Of course! And so it did.

The New Deal Legislation and Programs

It has been said that when Roosevelt took office he mounted his horse and galloped off in several directions at once. And really, that's sort of what he did. So many programs, each aimed at overcoming some visible problem, and some of the programs inconsistent and conflicting with each other—but there was no question that something was being done. *Action* was being taken.

The depression years of the Roosevelt administration are a truly unique period in American history. The things which happened during these few years brought major changes both in economics and in politics. The greatest changes were in the rapidly increasing functions of government in the economic system.

Many vital pieces of legislation were passed during the 1930s. It would be easy for you to spend an entire semester or an entire year studying the effects of the New Deal legislation on the economic system. Several books have been written about the changes wrought during these few hectic years. I hope that some day you will have the opportunity to study the interesting things that were going on then. But this book is not the place for that.

The purpose of this little book is to offer you perspective—an awareness of the rapid sweep of change in the evolution of society's economic processes and circumstances—and of the explosive rate of change in the world of yesterday, today, and tomorrow.

But you need a quick overview of the kinds of changes which were made by the New Deal legislation and programs. Many of the programs were temporary, but many initiated permanent changes in the nature of the economic system and in the role of government in the economy.

Roosevelt had to do several things *immediately.* He had to get the banks open again, and make the people confident that they would *remain* open. He had to somehow get some emergency funds to the state and local governments throughout the nation, almost all of which were in bad financial shape. And he had to get some food (or some money) into the hands of the unemployed and hungry people. All three of these objectives were worked on immediately.

The most difficult objective was getting money into the hands of people—getting them employed. The government started creating new money and undertaking all kinds of programs, including local conservation projects of all kinds and, later, public works projects. What to build? Build anything anybody can think of that seems to need to be built! Even if it didn't really need to be built, maybe it was better to build it than to leave the people unemployed. (Maybe someday some use for it could be figured out.)

The National Industrial Recovery Act

After the banks were reopened and the state and local governments were provided some emergency funds and the first steps were made toward overcoming starvation and unemployment, then attention was turned to the task of industrial recovery. The National Industrial Recovery Act was passed. It included "something for everybody."

The Act provided for minimum prices and production limits in agriculture; it permitted labor to unionize and bargain with employers; and it permitted the business firms in each industry to get together and work out a "code of fair competition," which, in effect, gave them monopoly power over outputs, marketing territories, prices, and other things.

Truly, the National Industrial Recovery Act (NIRA) was one of the most far-reaching pieces of legislation ever passed by the U.S. Congress. It was a radical departure from the concept of competition—in the agricultural markets, in the industrial-product markets, and in the labor markets. The NIRA was based on the idea that if everybody had enough *market power,* they could keep their prices up, thus keep their incomes up, thus keep their spending up, and thus assure prosperity in the economy.

The Act also established a public works program which provided for the construction of highways, dams, housing, post offices, other public buildings, water and sewer systems—any kind of public works project anyone could think of.

The NIRA, and the National Recovery Administration (NRA) which it created, lasted only about two years. In

1935 the Act was held unconstitutional by the Supreme Court. But soon, new acts were passed reestablishing and expanding many of the provisions of the NIRA. Agriculture markets were again placed under government control, and the monopoly powers of labor (to unionize and bargain and strike) were reaffirmed and strengthened. Many of the changes initiated in the NIRA were carried forward and still live on today.

Social Welfare Legislation

During the early days of the Roosevelt administration, emergency funds were provided to the state and local governments to bail out the welfare programs in the state and local areas. People needed relief, but the local governments didn't have much money for relief programs. Even with the federal grants the welfare programs couldn't meet the needs. Soon it was clear that the people wanted the government to take a stronger, more continuing role in providing for economic welfare.

In 1935, the Social Security Act was passed. This Act set up the old age and survivor's insurance program which has continued and been expanded repeatedly to the present time. This is a program of income redistribution: income from the wage earners (through social security taxes) and from the public (through taxes on businesses, which are ultimately paid by the public through higher product prices) is redistributed to people who are retired or disabled or sick or dependent survivors of wage earners. This is the OASDHI (Old Age Survivors Disability and Health Insurance) program that now redistributes billions of dollars of income every year.

In 1938, the Fair Labor Standards Act was passed, establishing minimum wages, setting the forty-hour workweek, and establishing various other "fair labor standards." This Act has also been continued and expanded to the present time.

The Full Employment Act of 1946

One of the most important pieces of New Deal legislation—legislation committing the government to an increased and continuing responsibility for the welfare of the people and for the functioning of the economy—was not passed until after the depression was over—not until the year after the sudden death of President Roosevelt in 1945. As World War II came to an end, many people were aware that massive government spending for the war had brought an end to the great depression. So now that the war was over, what was going to happen? Many people expected another depression. It was in this atmosphere that Congress passed the *Full Employment Act of 1946.*

This 1946 Act did not spell out any program. It simply stated that it is the continuing responsibility of the federal government to see to it that the economy will keep operating fast enough so that people can get jobs and incomes—so that employment and production and output will be maintained. If the economic system doesn't appear to want to run at the right speed on its own power, the government is responsible to do something to keep it running at the right speed. This Act set up the Council of Economic Advisers to keep the administration in touch with conditions in the economy, and to advise the President whenever action should be taken.

It would hardly be correct to say that following the years of the depression and World War II, laissez-faire was dead in the American economy. But certainly in many ways laissez-faire had been significantly reduced, and the influence of the political process on economic choices had been greatly expanded. Most of the changes that were made were more "pragmatic," trial-and-error changes than changes directed by either theory or philosophy.

But what were the economists doing all this time? If the economic theories couldn't help to explain what was going on and couldn't provide any guidelines as to what the government might do, then what were the economists doing?

You remember that back in the late 1800s economists weren't held in high esteem by laymen and policy makers because their "economic laws" didn't seem to be working in the real world. That's what happened again in the 1930s, when the accepted economic theories didn't seem to help to understand what was going on. But some economists were working on new explanations—trying to develop new ways of looking at and explaining what was going on in the world. The economist who made the greatest contribution—the one who has had the greatest impact on economic thinking in this century (perhaps in any century) was John Maynard Keynes (KAYNS). It's time now to talk about the evolution of economic ideas during the 1930s, and especially about the new ideas introduced by this brilliant and outspoken Englishman, Lord John Maynard Keynes.

THE NEOCLASSICAL THEORY OF DEPRESSION

The experience of the Great Depression made it obvious to all practical men that economists had some rethinking to do. Economists needed some new ways of looking at and explaining the economic forces at work in the modern industrial economic system of the twentieth century.

Neoclassical Economics Doesn't Address the Problem of Depression

Neoclassical economics didn't help much to explain what was happening during the 1930s. Economists, politicians, businessmen, *all* were trying to figure out how to get at and explain this new real-world happening: prolonged, persistent depression. To get at it, things had to be looked at in a new way.

For more than 100 years there have been times of boom and slump—some times when employment was high and wages were rising, prosperity was in the air; then other times when people found it hard to get jobs, incomes were low, and businesses had trouble surviving. These recurrent periods of prosperity and depression—these ups and downs of business—had been recognized as normal cycles in business activity. For a long time economists had been talking about and explaining these business cycles.

Business Cycles Were Natural and Self-Correcting

Neoclassical economics explained these recurrent depression periods as a necessary part of the system. There were several different theories, but all of them explained how a depression was a short-term, self-correcting condition—how depression conditions soon would move on into a period of recovery and then prosperity. But what about the 1930s? The U.S. economy (and the economies of most of the modern world) went into a devastating economic slump that just kept going on, year after year after year. What about that?

Neoclassical economics had no way to explain a decade of continuous depression. And without the massive government spending required by World War II, when might it have ended? And how? Neoclassical economics really didn't offer any good answers to these questions. Can you see that economists had some rethinking to do?

Neoclassical Economics Describes "the Market System at Work"

There must be a thousand different ways of looking at the world. And how you look at it determines what you will see. The classical and neoclassical economists looked at it as "a market system at work." They saw people buying things and they saw businesses producing the things people were buying. They saw the demand of the people controlling the uses of the society's resources. They saw everybody seeking more—workers seeking higher wages, landowners trying to get better rents, owners of money and capital trying to maximize their incomes, and businessmen working for maximum profits. They saw all these "owners of the factors of production" seeking more for themselves and thereby automatically responding to the demands of the society.

The businessman was supposed to make profits, then invest the profits and bring more economic growth. Competition was supposed to keep each businessman, each worker, each landowner, and everyone else doing the right things for the economy. Competition was to keep everyone in line. That's the way Adam Smith and the other classical economists, and Alfred Marshall and the other neoclassical economists looked at the world. And when they looked at it that way, of course that's what they saw.

Even the theories of Marx and the other radical critics of the laissez-faire market system were aimed in the wrong direction to help to explain the persistent, prolonged depression. Generally, *all* economists were concerned with the *interworkings of the parts* of the economic system. How do the pieces fit together? How are society's choices—about what to produce, how much of which things, which techniques of production to use, how much to put into capital and how much into consumer goods, how much each person will get as his "distributive share"—how are such choices made? These were the kinds of questions economists were trying to answer.

The Depression Question Wasn't Considered Relevant

To the classical and neoclassical economists, these "resource use, production, and distribution" questions *seemed* to be the relevant issues, since they thought the depression problem would take care of itself automatically. So they looked at the economic system in such a way as to bring them the kinds of answers they were looking for. But the 1930s presented the world with some new kinds of questions, and the old ways of looking at things didn't help much anymore.

With surplus farm commodities, prices were supposed to fall so that people would buy up the surpluses. With surplus workers, wages were supposed to fall so that more workers would be hired. With surplus industrial output, prices of products were supposed to fall until people would buy them all. With surplus savings, interest rates were supposed to go down until investors would borrow all the savings, and invest. All of the surpluses of everything—food, workers, products, money—were supposed to be automatically cleared away by falling prices. But that didn't happen. The surpluses persisted, while the economy slowed down more and more. Hungry people couldn't get the surplus food. People starved in the midst of plenty.

The goods weren't moving across the market. Why not? The otherwise very useful concepts of classical and neoclassical economics simply couldn't answer this kind of question. The neoclassical explanation of "how the system works" is just great—so long as the system is working. But when the system *breaks down* that's something else! And sure enough, the system had broken down.

Neoclassical economics has excellent explanations of *why* and *how* the market system works, and even of why it *must* work—why *it will not break down*. Then when the system *did* break down, of what help was neoclassical theory in explaining what had happened and why? No help. According to neoclassical theory it couldn't happen. The automatic price adjustments would not let it happen. But it *did* happen. If there was to be an explanation, it would have to come from some approach other than neoclassical economics.

Needed: A New Way of Looking at the Economy

Explanations of how the market functions when it is operating properly are not very helpful in understanding what's wrong when the market breaks down. In 1933, orthodox neoclassical economists may have been the *worst* people (rather than the best ones) to ask what was wrong, and what to do. They were looking at the world as a *functioning market system*. But the market system wasn't functioning. The neoclassical image of the world was no longer a helpful image. The world needed to be conceptualized differently—to be looked at in a different way. Think back.

Every era in history which has created a new set of conditions and problems has seen philosophers and activists arise to try to explain things and/or to change them—Adam Smith and Malthus and Ricardo and Saint Simon and Fourier and Robert Owen and Karl Marx and so many others—all arose more or less as products of their times. Each of them took on and tried to explain and/or change the real conditions of their day.

The 1930s gave us some new conditions. Some new issues. We needed some new ways to tackle them. We needed a new way of looking at the total economy—at what keeps it running, and at what makes it speed up, or slow down. We needed some new principles, some new theories. We needed to understand what is now called "macroeconomics." John Maynard Keynes came up with the new approach, the new principles and theories. He gave us a new way of looking at the economy, and he gave the world a good start toward finding some of the answers it was looking for.

THE ECONOMICS OF JOHN MAYNARD KEYNES

John Maynard Keynes finally gave the world a new way of looking at, and analyzing and explaining the depression problem. His book *The General Theory of Employment, Interest, and Money* (1936) offered some new ways of looking at the world and getting at the answers. He explained how it is possible for the economy to go into a persistent depression. And he explained what the government might do to overcome the depression.

Keynes offered some positive suggestions for what should be done. He didn't suggest (as neoclassical economists did) that we just suffer along and wait for the natural economic laws to work things out. The Keynesian *General Theory* recommended increased government spending, and it explained why more government spending was necessary.

The General Theory of Employment, Interest and Money (1936)

The first chapter of *The General Theory* consisted of a single paragraph in which Keynes slapped the economics profession in the face. Even now, almost forty years later, some economists are still smarting from the blow. What did Keynes say? Only that neoclassical economics didn't happen to fit the real world of the 1930s—that neoclassical economics was "misleading and disastrous" if we tried to use it to understand what was going on, and to guide public policy. Nothing timid about Keynes!

The economics profession scurried around trying to defend its position. But as time went on, more and more people came to accept "Keynesian economics" as valid—really, as an essential addition to our understanding of how the market system works in the real world. It was not that Keynesian economics invalidated neoclassical economics. Of course not. The most basic, most essential principles of economics are described and explained in neoclassical economics. But Keynes explained that there are times when that model—that way of looking at the world—is more *misleading* than helpful. Why? Because sometimes the real world doesn't behave the way the model *assumes* it will behave. When that happens, the neoclassical model may lead its followers off in exactly the *wrong* direction. That's what was happening in the 1930s.

Keynes Gave Us Macroeconomics

What Keynes did was comparable, in a way, to what Adam Smith had done about 160 years earlier. Keynes looked at the real world, he understood what he saw, and he gave us a way of seeing what was happening and why.

Keynes exhibited a rare understanding of the workings of the real world.

Most economists have exhibited much greater brilliance in dealing with models than in dealing with real-world issues and problems. But Keynes saw and understood the real world. And more than that. He had the unique ability to understand the real-world forces which influence and control the level of economic activity. He explained the forces which control the speed at which the economy operates. He built a theory explaining the depression—a theory which was aimed *directly* at the problem, and which offered avenues of *positive action* for dealing with it. Keynes gave us a way to understand the forces that influence the speed at which the economic system will run—that is, he gave us macroeconomics.

Keynes Earlier Writings

Keynes was about fifty years old when *The General Theory* appeared in 1936. But much earlier, before he reached thirty-five, he had indicated his ability to see and understand the economic realities of the world. In 1919 he wrote a book called the *Economic Consequences of the Peace.* In this book he explained why the World War I peace agreement was unworkable. The book was straight from the shoulder; it named names, and it left no doubt that Keynes thought the whole agreement proceeding was an exercise in stupidity. He said that the agreement would break down, and he predicted serious economic disruptions as a result. The book cost him some friends. But he was right, of course.

During the 1920s, Keynes was the editor of the *Economic Journal* (one of Britain's most honored economic publications), and he continued to criticize the government. In the mid-1920s, he attacked Britain's decision to return to the gold standard. He predicted that this move would be harmful to the nation, and that it would fail. But no one seemed to be listening. Again he was right, of course.

In 1930, Keynes published his two-volume *Treatise on Money.* This *Treatise* explained many of the concepts which later were integrated into his *General Theory.* But in 1930, no one was ready for a "new look" in economics. Everyone expected the depression to be short. Soon everything would be rolling along again. Keynes disagreed. He saw some serious fundamental problems. Some of these are explained in his *Treatise on Money.* Yes, he spoke out quite clearly. But at that time no one was listening very well.

As the years passed and the depression deepened, Keynes continued to give advice to government leaders. He wrote an open letter to President Roosevelt (published in the *New York Times* in 1933) and he served as occasional advisor to Roosevelt in the 1930s. In 1936 *The General Theory* was published. But it would not be until several years later that the thoughts expressed in that book would become integrated into the thinking of most economists.

Keynes at Bretton Woods

From the time *The General Theory* appeared in 1936 until his death ten years later, Keynes continued to play an active role as an adviser to governments on national and international policy. One of his last major involvements was in the Bretton Woods conferences (at Bretton Woods, New Hampshire) in 1945. There the postwar system of international exchange was worked out.

At Bretton Woods, Keynes suggested that some alternative to gold should be used in international finance. He suggested using some kind of "paper credits" instead of gold. But at that time the idea of using paper credits was just too far out. He predicted that the time would come when the world would have no choice but to move to some such system. And almost twenty-five years later the major nations agreed that it was essential to establish paper credits as an alternative to gold in balancing international financial accounts. A system of "special drawing rights" (SDRs) was initiated in the late 1960s and is still being worked out.

John Maynard Keynes was one of the greatest economists of all time. It isn't likely that any economist who ever lived had a clearer, more realistic understanding of how economics really works in the real world. Most of the economic concepts and principles we now call "macroeconomics" are Keynesian (and post-Keynesian or neo-Keynesian) economics. Most of today's macroeconomics has its roots in Keynes' *General Theory of Employment, Interest, and Money.*

We needed a new image of the world—a new way of looking at what was going on. A different perspective. John Maynard Keynes gave us that new perspective. His ideas have had a very real influence on the lives of all of us. No economic discussion, no prescription for attacking an economic problem, no economic policy has been quite the same since. Even those who have consistently opposed "the Keynesian way" of looking at the world have been unable to ignore Keynesian economics.

Keynesian Economics

What is Keynesian economics? It's a different way of looking at the world. It looks *directly* at the questions: What determines the *speed* of the economy? What determines *how much* (in total) will be produced? What determines whether or not all the labor, capital, land (the factors of production) will be employed as fully as their owners (and the society) want them to be employed?

Keynesian economics focuses attention on *the rate of spending* in the economy. Spending is what pulls forth the *output,* and thus supports *employment* and *incomes.* Keynesian economics seeks to explain what determines the level of total spending in the economy and what causes it to change. Keynesian economics tells us that if we can understand what determines the level of spending, we will know what determines the level of employment and production, of output and income in the economy.

Keynesian economics tells us that public policies which *change the level of spending* in the economy will *change the level of employment and production, and output and income* in the economy. Keynesian economics offers the government a *positive* approach to overcoming depression:

Make total spending increase and the economy will speed up. Increase government spending. Cut taxes so people and businesses will have more money to spend. Permit the money supply to expand. As the government and the businesses and the people all spend more, people all receive more. As people's incomes increase, their spending increases. The result: prosperity!

If the Keynesian prescription works, the economy will boom. Soon the government will need to cut down on its spending and raise taxes to keep the boom from running away into inflation.

The Market System Was "Flooded Out"

During the depression people were unemployed. They were receiving no income, so they weren't spending to buy anything. They couldn't buy anything because they didn't have any money to spend! The market process wasn't working.

The markets were sort of "flooded out." Surpluses existed in all the markets, but no one was buying the surpluses. Businesses weren't employing people. Why produce more when you can't sell what you already have? Everybody had lost confidence in the system. No one wanted to build new factories, homes, or anything else. Everybody took a defensive position—trying to hold on to what little bit of money they had for as long as they could. Not much money was being spent, so not much income was being received. The market system was "broken down."

Businesses went broke. Workers lost their jobs. They couldn't buy things. They couldn't pay the rent or make the car payments. Farmers couldn't sell their products. They went broke and couldn't buy tractors, gasoline, or fertilizer. The tractor, gasoline, and fertilizer companies had to cut back.

Banks couldn't collect on their loans. Many of the banks went broke. The moving finger of economic ruin touched each part, each unit in the economy—each household, each industry, each firm. Things just kept getting worse and worse. What was happening? And why? And what could be done? These are the questions that Keynesian economics came forward to answer.

Keynes Focused on the "Spending Sectors"

Keynes focused *directly* on the problem: not enough total spending. It's obvious that if the people and businesses and government are spending enough to buy up all the output of the economy, then the economy will keep producing: Full speed ahead! And it's just as obvious that when the total amount that the people and businesses and governments are buying *decreases,* then total output and employment will slow down. If businesses can't sell enough to keep all their workers busy, then they will lay off some workers. This obvious fact is what Keynes focused on.

Keynes analyzed total spending. He took it apart and looked at *who* was doing the spending, and why. Essentially, he split the "spending stream" into two sectors—spending for consumer goods, and spending for capital goods. Then he tried to get at the *motives* underlying each kind of spending—to try to see what underlies, what determines how much *each sector* of the spending stream will spend. If we can understand the *causes* of spending increases or decreases by each sector, then maybe we can induce total spending to adjust to the desired level. See what a neat approach Keynes thought of? (Like so many things, it seems quite obvious once someone else works it out and explains it to us!)

So Keynesian economics is the economics of under-standing *why* each sector of the spending stream (essentially consumers and businesses) spend as much as they do, and what makes their spending change. Also, Keynesian economics tries to explain how adjustments in government spending and taxes (and other things) can influence the total spending flow and thereby influence the speed at which the economy will run.

See the great importance of Keynesian (and neo-Keynesian) economics? It tells us how to prevent and how to overcome depressions! How? By doing things to keep total spending high enough to keep the economy prosperous.

The Pragmatic Keynesian Prescription

Once we focus on the *spending flow,* then the proper government policy to overcome depression becomes rather obvious: Spend more money. Do things to get businesses and consumers to spend more money. In a nutshell, this was the Keynesian prescription.

Much of what was done during Roosevelt's New Deal went along (more or less) with the Keynesian prescription—not because the actions were theoretically inspired, but because they were pragmatic—they seemed to be aimed in the right direction. When people are unemployed in every little town in the country, it's quite obvious that if the government will create enough money and spend it to hire all the unemployed people to build new post offices and other things, unemployment will be overcome. See how obvious and pragmatic the Keynesian prescription was? Maybe it wouldn't be too far off to say that Keynes gave Roosevelt and the Congress a theory to justify what Roosevelt and the Congress were already doing anyway!

Remember how that's sort of what Adam Smith did, too, for the industrialist capitalists—gave them a theory to justify what they were already doing anyway? Sure. It's interesting that the two men often referred to as the greatest economists of all time—Smith and Keynes—did not refine and make more precise the economist's theoretical models. Instead, they conceptualized and explained critical yet previously unexplained or inadequately explained conditions in the real world. Both left the refinements to the generations of economists who would follow.

World War II and Beyond

Did the Keynesian prescription work for Roosevelt? To some extent, maybe. It wasn't really tried. Not *really.* There were lots of anti-Keynesians around in the 1930s. The depression lingered on until the government began its really big military spending program for World War II. But once that began, the depression came to a rapid end. Almost immediately the government had to start working on the opposite problem. Shortages. Inflation. Tight controls were established on wages and prices. Most consumer goods and industrial products were placed under direct government allocation and carefully rationed among the competing high-priority uses.

After the war the economy kept on booming. What about the widely expected postwar depression? It never came. During the 1950s and '60s there were a few periods of economic slowdown (recessions) but never a threat of serious, prolonged depression. Technological progress was phenomenal—from propeller planes to trips to the moon in only about *two decades*—and from account books to modern electronic computers in less time than that. Truly phenomenal.

The later '40s and the '50s and '60s were generally good years in the U.S. and world economies. Not flawless, but not bad. Much progress was made. Most people were living better and better, having more things all the time. But quietly, mostly unnoticed, some serious problems were brewing. By the late '60s and early '70s the problems were ready to erupt and force themselves on the attention of the world. And so they did. The next chapter gives the highlights of how it all happened and tells what the economists were doing and thinking as they tried to keep up with this explosively changing world of the third quarter of the twentieth century.

5

THE MODERN WORLD: PROBLEMS OF UNEMPLOYMENT AND INFLATION

The Emergence of the New Economics
And the Challenge of Friedman
And the Monetarists

After World War II, the economy just kept on booming. The government cut back its spending, but consumers and businesses spent enough to more than make up the difference.

People Spent Their Wartime Savings and the Economy Boomed

During the war years, consumers had been denied the things they wanted while they were making good incomes. After the war was over, their savings, mostly in government bonds, were huge. So they cashed their bonds and bought the things they wanted—new houses, new automobiles, appliances, everything. Businesses invested in new plants and equipment and hired workers and tried to meet the strong *consumer* demand. This created a strong *business* demand. Total spending in the economy was high. Inflationary pressures were great. When the wartime price controls were removed, prices moved up. Inflation!

The Federal Reserve bought the bonds that the people, businesses, and banks were cashing, pouring money into the economy. The new money went into the banks, creating new reserves, permitting the money supply to expand rapidly. Then in 1949 demand slacked some, relieving the inflationary pressures. But in 1950 the Korean War caused government spending to increase, and prices again began moving upward rapidly. So what happened? Price and wage controls were imposed. The controls were kept on until the end of the war.

The Economy Was Sluggish During the Late 1950s

During the eight years of the Eisenhower administration (1953–1960) the economy experienced three recessions. Growth was not as rapid as many economists thought it should be. During much of the period, unemployment was higher than most economists considered necessary. As the Eisenhower administration was coming to an end, the economy was suffering a fairly serious recession—the worst of the postwar era. In this setting John F. Kennedy was elected president.

THE EVOLUTION OF NEO-KEYNESIAN ECONOMICS

Kennedy entered the White House with the pledge to "get the economy moving again." During the Kennedy–Johnson era the theories of neo-Keynesian economics ("neo-Keynesian" meaning the ideas of Keynes, as further developed by other economists in the 1940s, '50s, and '60s) first were fully relied on to guide public policy. But before we get into that we need to talk about how the neo-Keynesian ideas were evolving in the postwar period.

The Keynesian Prescription: Unbalance the Budget

The basic idea of the Keynesian prescription for overcoming unemployment and depression was to unbalance the government budget. The government would reduce its "tax withdrawals" from the income stream at the same time it would increase its "spending injections" into the income stream. The idea was for the government to unbalance the budget, to run a deficit, to create more money to finance its expenditures, and push more money into the spending and income flow of the economy. How was this idea of unbalancing the budget on purpose received following World War II?

Many economists accepted the Keynesian prescription in the 1940s and '50s, but *public policy* did not fully reflect this attitude. Many politicians, congressmen, businessmen and ordinary citizens had strong "balance the budget" attitudes. During the sluggish years of the 1950s there was no purposeful budget unbalancing to try to speed up the economy.

The Neo-Keynesian Prescription: The "New Economics"

It was not until the early 1960s—actually, not until 1963, the year of President Kennedy's death—that neo-Keynesian economics was explicitly stated as public policy. It was stated by President Kennedy at the Harvard graduation in June 1963. This is the basic idea of what he said:

> Even though we are already running a government deficit, we are going to cut taxes and even further unbalance the budget. The economy will be so stimulated by the tax cut that soon people and businesses will be making so much more income that they will be paying much *more* to the government in income (and other) taxes. The extra *tax revenues* will be big enough to bring the budget into balance.

A radical idea, right? Cut taxes in order to collect more taxes? Wow! (The idea was that *raising taxes* to try to balance the budget—which was what the Eisenhower administration had done—would only slow down the economy even more and make the deficit *larger!*)

What had happened during the years following World War II, to prepare the nation to accept such a radical idea—the idea of *further* unbalancing the budget *on purpose*; the idea that *cutting* taxes will produce more revenue than *raising* taxes? What had happened to ready the policymakers for such an unorthodox economic policy? Such a policy would have been considered nonsense only a few years earlier. What brought about the change in thinking?

The Synthesis of Keynesian Economics into
Orthodox Economics

Perhaps the most important influence was the synthesis, or integration, of Keynesian economics into the general body of accepted economic principles. As time went on, most economists (and apparently most people) came to accept Keynesian economics—not as a substitute for, but as a necessary complement to neoclassical economics. How did it happen? Probably the greatest influence was Professor Paul Samuelson's *Economics* book.

Samuelson's *Economics* (first edition, 1947) did an exceptionally good job of explaining the ideas and principles of Keynesian economics, not to the *exclusion* of, but *together with* the orthodox principles of evolving neoclassical economics.

Samuelson's book was widely used, and soon widely imitated. Even today, more than a quarter-century later, the Samuelson book (now in its ninth edition) and other, similar books are the ones used to introduce most economics students to the concepts and principles of economics.

During the 1950s and '60s most of the graduates pouring out of the colleges and going into business or public administration or law or politics or most other worldly pursuits had been exposed to Keynesian economics. Most of them had some understanding of the Keynesian (neo-Keynesian) prescription for overcoming unemployment and recession and for keeping the economy running along at a proper clip.

See what happened? So many people understood the ideas and principles that Keynesian economics wasn't so mysterious any more! An increasing number of leading citizens were able to understand the Keynesian prescription and to call on the government to apply it to speed up the economy.

Neoclassical Economics and the Post-Keynesian Synthesis

Exactly what was this post-Keynesian synthesis?—this integration of neo-Keynesian and neoclassical ideas? Quite simple, really. The neoclassical model was still accepted as a valid statement of the *market forces* which are constantly at work in the society. But the post-Keynesians recognized that there were many other forces, too—forces *outside* the neoclassical model—some outside of *economics* even—which sometimes would be strong enough to overpower the neoclassical market forces—maybe even carry the world in the *opposite* direction. And when that happened, the neoclassical model would be not the best but the *worst* place to look for an explanation. That's when the concepts and principles of neo-Keynesian economics were needed.

The Focus of Neoclassical Economics. Neo-Keynesian economics is based on a different set of assumptions than neoclassical economics. Neoclassical economics focuses on the forces which, if left free to operate without impediment, will always bring the economy fairly quickly and smoothly into a "long-run equilibrium" of full employment and stable prices, with all resource uses optimized—that is, all labor, land, and capital directed in the most efficient ways toward the true objectives of the society. A beautiful system! Unfortunately, in the real world it doesn't work out quite that way.

The Focus of Neo-Keynesian Economics. The post-Keynesians also believe in the neoclassical model as an essential tool for explaining what the market forces are and how they work. But they don't believe those forces always work out in the same predictable ways. They don't believe in the "inevitable mechanistic determination" of real-world economic events, as described in the neoclassical model. They don't believe that the normal real-world economic condition always looks like the long-run equilibrium of the neoclassical model. Therefore, when they see high unemployment and other signs that the economy isn't running as it should, they look to the ideas of neo-Keynesian economics to help them to understand what's going on.

Neo-Keynesian economics focuses on the spending flow—on what speeds it up and what slows it down—and on what the government can do to influence the spending flow. The spending flow is what supports employment, production, and prices. When it slows down, the economy slows down. Recession.

As an economy grows and prospers, people's incomes go up. People with high incomes save a lot. They may pull so much savings out of the income stream that a depression will result. Prices may not easily adjust to end the depression as the neoclassical model says they will. That's when Keynesian economics is helpful in understanding what's going on, and in deciding what to do about it.

The government should *take action*. Follow the Keynesian prescription. Spend enough to offset the savings. Or cut taxes so people and businesses will be able to spend more. Or promote "easy money" (low interest rates) so businesses and people may borrow and spend more.

Many economists with widely differing views can be grouped together under the post-Keynesian label. Almost all economists these days agree with some of the neo-Keynesian ideas. John F. Kennedy was the first U.S. President to publicly announce his commitment to Keynesian economics.

The Kennedy Tax Cut

It was in 1963 that Kennedy called on Congress for a tax cut, but it was not until 1964 that the tax cut actually came.

And did it work? Apparently it really did! The economy really did speed up, and tax revenues really did *increase.* The American economy enjoyed an unprecedented period of prosperity and growth. But some economists were critical. They didn't think the tax cut *caused* the prosperity. It's true that there were many things going on, influencing the economy in the mid-'60s. One thing was the Vietnam war. We'll talk more about that soon, but first, here's something else to think about.

The Keynesian Prescription Gives People Confidence

Throughout the '50s and early '60s almost everyone who took economics in college learned about the Keynesian prescription. Everyone learned that the government knew how to prevent a serious depression. Perhaps people's *confidence* that the economy was depression-free actually helped to make the economy depression-free. Consider this: As long as people are confident that depression won't come, depression can't come! Did people's understanding of the Keynesian prescription help to stabilize the economy during the '50s and '60s? Nobody knows for sure, of course. But it's interesting to think about.

We know that as long as people expect times to be good, times will be good. But if enough people *expect* bad times—either inflation or depression—then that's exactly what we will have. People *spend now,* to protect themselves from inflation. Their increased spending brings shortages, and soon we have the inflation they feared. People *save* to protect themselves from depression. When people save more (spend less), businesses don't sell as much. They cut back production and lay off workers. So what happens? Depression. See how it works? As people try to protect themselves from inflation or depression, they only bring on or worsen the inflation or the depression they're worrying about!

Confidence is essential. Yet without *Keynesian economics,* what prescription can the economist offer as "economic stabilization insurance"? None. Without Keynesian economics we are right back where we were before the depression of the 1930s, with no way to prescribe effective action to revitalize the system. So who, pray tell, would throw out Keynesian economics? Milton Friedman and all the other *monetarists,* that's who. Why? Because they don't think it's needed. And they don't think it works.

THE CHALLENGE TO NEO-KEYNESIAN ECONOMICS

In the way the monetarists perceive the world, Keynesian economics is unnecessary, irrelevant, wrong, harmful. If the monetarists' perception of the world is correct, then Keynesian economics *is* wrong and harmful. But if the monetarists' perception of the world is *not* correct, then the monetarists are doing mankind serious harm by discrediting these prescriptive tools for dealing with economic instability, economic stagnation, and depression.

The Anti-Keynesians: Milton Friedman and the Monetarists

Throughout the period of the 1940s, '50s, and '60s, while Keynesian economics was being integrated into the mainstream of economic understanding, a few economists were speaking out loud and clear against Keynesian economics and against the whole idea of government fiscal policy—of adjusting taxes and spending to influence the economy. The leading challengers have been (and are) Milton Friedman and his colleagues who make up "the Chicago School" of economic thought—or, more specifically, the "monetarist" school of economic thought.

Friedman and his followers weren't the first monetarists. Far from it! The philosopher David Hume, one of Adam

Smith's contemporaries, fairly well explained this idea more than two hundred years ago—and even Hume was not the first to explain it. Then in the early 1900s the Yale University economist Irving Fisher took up the cause and further refined the theory. In the 1920s the Stable Money Association was formed to push forward Fisher's ideas. Here's the basic idea:

A change in the *size* of the *money supply* is the thing that causes *prices* to change. If the money supply increases, people have more money to spend. So they start buying more things. Soon shortages appear. People have money but can't find the things they want to buy. So they start offering *more* to get what they want. Prices start going up. This process continues until prices are high enough to bring everything back into balance again. If the money supply doubles, prices will double. It's as simple as that.

It works the other way, too. If the money supply decreases, people will have less money to spend, so they will buy less. Surpluses will begin piling up in the markets. Business will slow down. There will be a (temporary) depression. Sellers will cut prices so they can sell all their products. Workers will work for lower wages so they can get jobs. Banks will lend for lower interest so they can get investors to borrow. *All* prices come down (by varying amounts) until everything is back in balance and the economy is humming along again.

The public policy implication of the basic monetarist idea is obvious: Keep the money supply the right size and everything will be all right. An expanding money supply brings rising prices. It's inevitable! A contracting money supply brings falling prices. It's inevitable!

The Neoclassical, Monetarist Prescription: Hands Off!

So what do Milton Friedman and the monetarists of the Chicago School have to say about the new economics—that is, about the neo-Keynesian prescription for influencing the economy? They disagree strongly. The monetarists insist that neoclassical economics is all we need. If the *money supply* is properly adjusted, spending and prices and employment will adjust automatically and the economy will run properly.

To the monetarists, there's just no need to get involved with the Keynesian prescription. To do so would do more harm than good. The government's *only* economic policy should be to control the size of the money supply and its rate of increase. As total output and trade increase, the money supply should be permitted to increase enough to finance the increased trade. But that's all. The government should keep taxing and spending in proper balance, should work out flexible international exchange rates so international trade can come into natural balance, and should keep the money supply expanding at about 5 percent per year. Those are the *only* economic stabilization policies the government should have. Beyond that, the policymakers should just relax and let nature take its course.

Even the neoclassical monetarist members of the Chicago School admit that the neoclassical model doesn't work out *exactly right* in the real world. But they think it comes out close enough. And they think that if public policy follows the Keynesian prescription or tries in any other way to influence the economy, things will be made worse—not better.

To the modern neoclassical monetarists, economic events are to a very large extent *mechanistically determined*—that is, determined by the natural forces of the market mechanism (the forces of demand and supply and price) which are so clearly illustrated in the neoclassical model. The natural laws of economics determine what result will follow from each cause. Any attempts by government to alter the results would interfere with the natural forces and therefore would be harmful, and doomed to failure. Holding these beliefs, it's no wonder the monetarists try to discredit Keynesian economics!

The Monetarist Creed: Keep Your Eye on the Money Supply

According to Milton Friedman and his followers, the government should never take any kind of direct discretionary action to influence employment or spending or wages or prices. The 5 percent limit on expansion of the money supply will take care of the problem of inflation; automatic price adjustments and the automatic forces of the market system will take care of unemployment and depression. The government shouldn't do anything to try to make the economy run better than it runs naturally. Any action the government takes to try to improve things will only make matters worse.

"Keep your eye on the money supply. Let everything else alone. If times are bad, there's nothing the government can do. If the government tries to do something it will only slow down the natural adjustments and delay the coming of good times. The government has no business fooling around with the economy." So say Milton Friedman and his colleagues, the monetarists.

The Effects of Friedman Economics on Public Policy

What effect has "Friedman economics" had on U.S. public policy? Perhaps a little during the Eisenhower administration, but certainly none during the Kennedy-Johnson era. During the Kennedy-Johnson era, excessive inflationary pressures were dealt with by direct government influence. Wage-price guideposts were set up and the power of the presidency was used to coerce businesses and labor into going along with these guideposts. This general approach came to be known as "jawboning"—an unofficial but usually quite effective technique of arm-twisting to prevent labor and businesses from getting big wage or price increases.

Then, when Nixon took office in January of 1969, the scene changed. President Johnson's economic advisers were replaced. President Nixon spoke out strongly against any kind of direct controls—jawboning or otherwise. The Congress passed a law giving him legal powers to establish direct controls on wages and prices. But Nixon vowed that he would never use those powers. He vowed, right in the beginning and repeatedly thereafter, that as long as he was President no direct controls would be imposed. His advisers assured him that holding down the size of the money supply would solve the inflation problem and that no direct controls would ever be necessary.

President Nixon was very slow to change his mind. But as things turned out he did change his mind. Let's go back to the 1950s and trace the events step by step so you can see how it all happened.

THE EVOLUTION OF THE CURRENT
INFLATION PROBLEM

Back in the 1950s, after the Korean War ended (1953), the wartime wage-price controls were abolished. There was a minor recession; inflation didn't seem to be a problem. But then as the years went by, prices began to creep upward. When prices were increasing at about 2 percent a year, money was "tightened up" to hold down the rate of inflation. But when money was tightened, the economy slowed down.

When the economy slowed down, the government budget automatically went into a deficit. (Tax payments drop sharply when total income falls, of course.) In 1957–58 the economy went into a recession. The Eisenhower administration tried to balance the budget—to hold down public spending, and keep tax collections high. But the budget deficits continued, and the economy stayed in recession. There was some improvement in 1958–1959, but in 1960–61 things got worse again. In January 1961, when President Kennedy took office, unemployment was approaching 7 percent.

Walter Heller and the New Economics

Not until the early years of the Kennedy administration (1961–62) did the economy begin to pick up. But still, unemployment was high. In 1963, Walter Heller, Chairman of President Kennedy's Council of Economic Advisers, persuaded Kennedy to apply the Keynesian prescription to try to speed up the economy. Thus, for the first time Keynesian economics began to play a dominant role in influencing economic policy for the nation. Walter Heller was the chief spokesman for this neo-Keynesian approach, which came to be called "the new economics."

One idea of the new economics is that if the government tries to balance its budget when the economy is running too slowly the economy will be prevented from reaching full speed. When the economy is underemployed, the government *should* run a deficit. It should set tax rates at that level at which the budget will come into balance *automatically* whenever the economy gets up to "full employment." If the economy gets "overheated"—too much spending and inflation—tax revenues will increase automatically, the budget will run a surplus, and that will hold down the excess spending.

In 1958 when the economy slowed down, the U. S. government ran the biggest peacetime budget deficit in history. When the Eisenhower administration tried to balance the budget, the economy just stagnated and the budget still didn't balance. But in 1964 when the deficit was more than $8 billion, the Kennedy administration *lowered* taxes. (President Kennedy asked Congress for the tax cut back in the summer of 1963. It was slow in coming. Congress doesn't always jump and run just when the President asks, of course!)

What happened after the Kennedy tax cut of 1964? The economy sped up. Unemployment dropped. Incomes rose. The deficit dropped from $8 billion in 1964 to $5 billion in 1965. Why? Individuals and businesses were making higher incomes, so they were paying more taxes. That's what reduced the deficit.

The booming economy helped almost everybody. State and local governments received more tax revenues, so they could do a better job of providing education and other public services. Monetary policy was "easy"—interest rates were kept low and the money supply was allowed to expand to finance the boom. Everything seemed to be going just fine. Then suddenly there was a new problem: the Vietnam war.

Spending for the Vietnam War Broke the Balance

U. S. involvement in the war expanded slowly, then more rapidly, until soon the war was making heavy demands on the economy. Government spending poured into the nation's income stream. As the government demanded more war goods, shortages developed in some markets. When the economy is "fully employed" and the government uses more of the nation's labor, resources, and products, the people must do with less. Taxes should be raised to get the people to buy less. Otherwise: Shortages. Inflation.

President Johnson and his Council of Economic Advisers urged Congress to increase taxes to pull some of the money back out of the economy to hold down total spending. But Congress did not act. (Voting to raise taxes is not a very popular thing for a congressman to do.) So what happened? Prices began to rise. Of course.

How much extra spending was the government pumping into the economy? In 1967 the deficit approached $9 billion. In 1968 it was $25 billion! What to do? Antiwar sentiment was growing. Many Congressmen refused to vote for increased taxes to finance the war. Finally, in 1968, there was a tax increase. But it was too little and too late. The inflation fires were already ablaze.

Prices had been increasing for several years at a rate of around 3 percent a year. The inflation rate picked up a little in 1968, but it wasn't until 1969, the first year of the Nixon administration, that prices began to break loose and run. In 1969 prices were increasing at an annual rate of about 6 percent. Nixon vowed that he would bring inflation under control. What did his Friedmanesque economic advisers prescribe? Tight money, of course.

Remember the slogans? "Keep your eye on the money supply." "When inflation threatens, hold tight on the money supply." "If the money supply is not permitted to expand too much, then it follows as the night the day, prices cannot rise too much." That's what the economic advisers prescribed; and that's exactly what the Nixon administration did—at least that's what it started out to do, and tried to do.

Nixon's "Tight Money Policy" Didn't Work as Expected

The Federal Reserve (Fed) held back on credit. The Fed refused to let the money supply continue to expand. That was the only action the administration took. Soon there was such a shortage of money that interest rates rose to levels higher than they had been in the United States for more than one-hundred years. The stock market collapsed—the worst tumble in stock prices since the depression years of the 1930s. And what about prices? Did tight money stop inflation? No.

Prices kept on increasing faster and faster. Also unemployment increased more and more—from 4 percent to 5 percent, then, in 1971, to more than 6 percent. Tight money, plus some slowdown in government buying, forced the economy into a recession. But prices kept on rising. Inflation kept getting worse.

More and more, people were criticizing the Nixon administration's economic policy. Many urged Nixon to stop relying entirely on his indirect, "theoretical" approach. They urged him to go beyond the monetarist approach and beyond the neo-Keynesian approach—to take some *direct* action to break the wage-price spiral. Many suggested direct controls on wages and prices to break the inflation, after which perhaps more normal policy tools could be used to keep things stabilized.

In 1970 Congress passed the Act giving the President the power "to impose such orders and regulations as he may deem appropriate to stabilize prices, rent, wages, and salaries. . . ." But the President repeatedly asserted that he would never use this authority—that he would never use the power of his office to force direct controls over wages and prices. But as everyone knows, history was to prove him wrong.

Early in 1971 it appeared that things were beginning to get better. The economy seemed to be picking up a little and Nixon's economic advisers kept assuring everyone that the tight money anti-inflation policies were just about ready to take hold. But then in the summer of 1971 things took a dramatic turn for the worse.

People Lost Confidence in Nixon's Policies

Unemployment had continued to hover around 6 percent. Consumer spending was slow and was not picking up. Prices just kept on increasing faster and faster. During the early part of 1971 wholesale prices were rising at a record rate. The stock market (which had recovered somewhat) went back into a tailspin. It was clear that economic conditions were getting worse, not better. The deficit in the U.S. international balance of payments kept getting worse. More and more dollars were pouring into the bank accounts of foreigners. And more and more of these dollar holders began to try to get rid of their surplus of dollars. But no one wanted to hold *more* dollars. The international value of the dollar seemed almost certain to go down.

For more than two years President Nixon and his advisors had been promising repeatedly that the economy was going to correct itself very soon. But as the weeks, months, and years passed and none of the promises came true, people began to suspect that the Nixon economists really didn't understand as much as they said they did. The medicine they kept applying seemed to be doing much harm and no good. It was in the spring and summer of 1971 that the business and financial community and many of the political leaders, both in the United States and throughout the world, lost confidence in Nixon's economic policy. The problems were getting rapidly worse, threatening serious domestic and international consequences. Something had to be done.

Nixon's Abrupt Shift in Policy

In his historic television address on Sunday night, August 15, 1971, President Nixon announced what is probably the most sudden shift of economic policy that has ever occurred in this country. He placed an immediate freeze on wages and prices, announced his recommendations to Congress for tax cuts and other actions to stimulate spending, and announced that the dollar would be devalued—that is, sold cheaper to people in other countries.

Why this absolute reversal in policy? It was obvious that something had to be done. Quickly. Regardless of Nixon's philosophical leanings and the continued urging of most of his advisers (some of whom had deserted the Nixon "game plan" before he did), he knew that something immediate, direct, *dramatic,* had to be done—Nixon the pragmatist, the opportunist, realized this. When he moved, he moved decisively. Most of the world applauded his decisive intervention. Most of his critics criticized him not for what he did, but because he had waited so long, had "let so many horses out of the stable" before taking any direct action. We'll talk about what happened under the freeze, and under all of the phases that followed; but first, here's a look at what was going on with the American dollar in the international exchange markets of the world.

Foreigners Lost Confidence in the Dollar

As prices were spiraling upward in the American economy, what was happening to the value (the purchasing power) of the dollar? It was spiraling downward. If prices double, then the dollar will only buy half as much. That means, in *real* terms, the dollar is only *worth* half as much as before.

Foreigners hold billions of American dollars. Foreign banks, businesses, and individuals have bank accounts in American banks and hold American bonds and other "dollar assets." Why? Because ever since World War II—until recent years—the dollar had been a very good asset to hold—in fact, "as good as gold." Foreigners could actually use their dollars to buy gold from the U. S. government, so their dollars really were as good as gold.

As long as prices in the United States are going up only slightly (prices in most other countries were going up more rapidly), the dollar was just great as an asset to hold. But when prices in the United States began spiraling upward, it became obvious that the dollar wasn't such a desirable asset anymore. So people holding dollars began to want to get rid of them, to trade them for gold, or for some other kind of money—money less likely to depreciate in value so fast.

Another thing was happening, too. As prices of American products spiraled upward, American buyers saw opportunities to buy foreign products *cheaper.* So they did. American consumers began buying more and more German cars and Japanese cars and tape recorders. Businesses began buying more Japanese steel. As time went on the flood of products from foreign countries increased. Each time an American bought a foreign product, more dollars flowed into the bank accounts of the foreigners. This gave the foreigners more dollars to try to get rid of.

In the spring and summer of 1971 this desire to get rid of dollars began to assume panic proportions. Foreigners who held dollars were getting more and more nervous, more and more ready to sell their dollars to anyone who would buy them, with marks, or yen, or some other currency—some kind of money they could believe in. (The U. S. government had long since stopped selling gold to just anyone who wanted it, but they had been selling to the central banks of other countries. During the early 1970s gold was flowing to other countries by the billions.

The rapidly expanding international payments deficit and the rapid gold drain made it absolutely imperative that President Nixon take some action immediately. Perhaps the inflationary spiral could have been suffered for a bit longer. Perhaps—except for the international plight of the dollar— the tight money game plan might have been continued for a while. But as the American dollar was becoming unacceptable to foreigners, some actions were imperative. Nixon had no choice.

The Dollar Was Devalued

On August 15, 1971, when President Nixon announced the wage-price freeze he also announced that no longer would gold be sold to *anyone,* and he announced the devaluation of the dollar—that is, that it would be sold cheaper (for less foreign money) in the future. At first the dollar was going to be allowed to "float." That means anyone who wanted to sell dollars would have to sell them for whatever they could get from whoever wanted to buy them. Official exchange rates for the dollar were temporarily abandoned.

With official exchange rates, American tourists abroad who had traveler's checks and American dollars knew just how many francs, or marks, pounds, lire, kroner, drachmas, yen, or any other currency they could get for a given number of dollars. But after August 15, the tourist who went into the foreign bank for currency never knew how much he was going to get. But one thing he knew for sure—he was going to get less than he would have gotten before!

What were the effects of the devaluation and other moves to strengthen the dollar? Did they work? To some extent, yes. But as time went on it became clear that the balance of payments problem had not been solved. In 1972 and 1973 the international problem of the dollar continued, more acute sometimes than at other times. Attempts were made to put together a new system of exchange rates, but without success. In early 1974 the dollar strengthened considerably, but at the time this book goes to press (spring 1974) the future of international exchange rates and of the international role of the dollar is still very much in question.

The Phases of the Nixon Wage-Price Control Policies

The wage-price freeze of August 15, 1971, was an absolute freeze for ninety days on all wages and prices. When the freeze (Phase I) ended, Phase II began. Under Phase II, wage and price adjustments were permitted, but only within the limits of established guidelines. As the months went by, it became clear that the inflationary spiral indeed had been broken. Wages and prices were rising moderately. Confidence in the economy was being regained.

Milton Friedman, leader and most steadfast of all monetarists, criticized the control program, saying that the inflationary spiral *really* had been brought under control by the delayed action of the administration's tight money policies. Friedman said that if the controls hadn't been put on, conditions would be *even better!* Of course, no one except his most devout disciples believed him.

What about President Nixon? Did he believe Friedman? Maybe so. In January of 1973, fourteen months after the beginning of Phase II, Nixon lifted the Phase II controls. So what happened? In the months that followed, the American economy experienced the worst inflation since 1946. The massive rush of foreigners to get rid of their dollars was *the worst* in the history of the nation. Soon the dollar was devalued two more times.

Exactly what did Nixon do in January 1973? He announced the beginning of Phase III. The ending of mandatory controls. He wanted to move to voluntary guidelines. Obviously people didn't believe it would work, and obviously it didn't. So what did Nixon do next?

In June of 1973 the President announced another freeze, which soon became known as Phase three-and-a-half. We were almost back again to Phase I—back to August 1971—except now in a much worse position. Prices were much higher, and confidence in the government's ability to cope with the situation was much lower than before. In addition, the Watergate scandal was eroding domestic and international confidence in the Nixon administration, and the energy crisis and shortages of other basic resources were beginning to push upward on prices.

A month after the June freeze, Phase IV was announced. Phase IV looked a lot like Phase II, except that prices were "unfrozen" in stages—some in July, some in August, and some in September. As prices were unfrozen they were permitted to rise, but *only* enough to cover increases in *costs*. Some prices—notably the prices of unprocessed agricultural commodities—were left free to respond to the forces of supply and demand.

What Happens Next?

What does the future hold in store? Will wage and price increases be held to "tolerable" rates? Will international confidence in the dollar be strong enough to permit a new, stable system of international exchange rates to be developed? No one knows. A lot depends on public confidence in the administration's economic policies. If the people expect a control program to fail, very likely it *will* fail. As this book goes to press, public confidence in the administration is low. It will be interesting (maybe scary!) to watch what happens next.

What about the long run? Can direct controls be eliminated someday? And everything go along just fine, with no controls after that? Of course not. The American economy and the other economies of the world have strong "built in" inflationary pressures which will *require* some continuing government restraints on wages and prices. Does this mean that fiscal and monetary controls will be unnecessary? Of course not!

Direct controls can't work unless the money supply and the government budget are held in check. But it seems that monetary and fiscal controls sometimes are not enough. Holding down "demand pressures" in the economy—by holding down the money supply (and total spending)—is a *necessary* condition but not always a *sufficient* condition for controlling inflation. Too many people have too much "autonomous power" over the prices of things. Just holding down money and spending is likely to cause depression before it stops inflation. Most people seem to know that now.

The Neoclassical Model Doesn't Describe the Real World

From the economic policy history of the first five years of the Nixon administration it would seem that everyone must have learned this lesson: The modern economic system is *not* the neoclassical pure competition model. It's something quite different.

The forces of the model really are at work in the real world, of course. But those forces aren't the *only* forces at work. To assume so is naive. To base national economic policy on such an assumption is irresponsible and dangerous. Surely everyone must have learned by now that *direct restraints* on wages and prices are an essential part of the government's "full employment and stable prices" tool kit. Ideologically distasteful? To some people, perhaps. But *essential* just the same.

Chronic Inflation: One of Modern Society's Urgent Problems

Chronic inflation is one of the serious, urgent economic problems of modern society. Our public policies for controlling it are not adequate. Our theories explaining it are not adequate. It seems likely that society is destined to suffer more than necessary as the "anti-inflation" policy makers waver between the conflicting views and advices of their quarreling economic advisors.

Chronic inflation isn't the only serious economic problem of the modern world. It's time now to look at some others—at the issues of giant corporations, environmental destruction, and the way the modern economies of mixed capitalism are evolving as they try to cope with these and other problems of modern society. That's the subject of the next chapter.

THE MODERN WORLD: MONOPOLY, ECOLOGY, AND THE "SOCIALIZATION OF CAPITALISM"

New Problems, New Theories, and the Rapid Evolution of Economic Society

The preceding chapter was concerned with the issues of depression and inflation, employment and prices, during the three decades since World War II. These issues were, and still are, very serious. But there were also some other serious issues emerging during this period. This chapter talks about some of them.

The economic power of giant businesses has been increasing—some say increasing *too much* for the good of society. The explosive growth in industrialization and population threatens the environment. *Resource use* and *waste disposal*, already excessive, are increasing rapidly—at rates which are intolerable for the long run. We need to take a quick look at each of these urgent problems: giant businesses, and the ecological balance between modern industrial society and its worldly environment.

GIANT BUSINESSES AND THE QUESTION OF SOCIAL CONTROL

Remember how the market system is supposed to work? Adam Smith and the other classical economists explained it.

Alfred Marshall and the other neoclassical economists explained it. It works through consumer demand, and competition among sellers. All the sellers try to make more profit by trying to outdo each other in serving the consumer. That way the society's wishes are served, and the producers are controlled by the demands and preferences of the buyers. We might say: "The society controls its economy through the *market process."*

But what happens when big business comes into the picture? Suppose there's only one seller of a product. And suppose the product is one that most people feel is pretty essential. Since there aren't any competing sellers, the seller may not bother to improve his product. He may not bother to produce as much as the people would like. He may let shortages develop, and with shortages, he can raise his price, make more profits. He can get *rewarded* for doing a *disservice* to society.

This is the point: Competition is essential if the market system is to work right. As businesses get larger and larger, and hold larger and larger shares of various markets, they have more and more power to control the markets in their own interest. They don't have to be so careful about responding to the interest of the buyers. Essentially, that is the problem of big business—of monopoly.

The Continuing Growth of Big Business

Back in the last century, big businesses were growing by leaps and bounds. The Sherman Antitrust Act was passed in 1890 to try to hold down the growth of monopoly in the markets of the American economy. But the Sherman Act didn't seem to help much. More antimonopoly laws were passed in the early 1900s. Additional laws have been passed from then until now. The laws and the courts have had a considerable effect in nipping the growth and exercise of monopoly power. But still there's a lot of big business around. How big? And how bad are its effects? And what's going to be done about it? These are tough questions.

Back in the 1930s many people were concerned about big business. A study showed that about one-half of all the corporate wealth in the United States was concentrated in the hands of some two-hundred companies. And what has happened since that time? This concentration of corporate wealth has increased even more. If we look only at *industrial* corporations (eliminating the transportation and utility companies), the pattern of increasing concentration of corporate wealth in the hands of a few is easy to see. In 1929, about one-fourth of all industrial corporate wealth was in the hands of the top one-hundred corporations. By the early 1960s that figure had grown to about one-third. By 1970, it had increased to about *one-half.*

Mergers, and the Growth of Multinational Corporations

There is no question that the big corporations, the ones that have been doing well, have been doing *very* well. They have been gathering more and more assets by merging other companies into their "parent corporations." Great amounts of corporate wealth are being concentrated in the hands of a relatively small number of corporations, not just in the United States but worldwide, both with big corporations in other countries and with the rapid growth of the multinational corporation.

If the big, multinational corporations were to grow over the next several years as they have been in the last several years (which does not seem likely), in about fifteen or twenty years almost all of the production in the world would come from three-hundred big worldwide firms, two-hundred of which would be U. S.-based corporations.

Can you see that this concentration of wealth in the hands of a few corporations might be something for economists to worry about? Can a national or world economy made up of a few massive corporations be expected to follow the laws of economics as defined in the neoclassical economist's model economy, made up of great numbers of small, competitive businesses? Of course not!

We Have No Accepted Theory of the Big Business Economy

Certainly there are advantages to bigness in business: planning and stability, long-range goals and willingness to make long-range commitments for research and development; and perhaps the development of a "social consciousness," which in modern economic systems in the real world may be an essential function. But one thing is certain: These big firms will not operate the way the small, very competitive firms of the neoclassical model are—in theory—*supposed* to operate. So how do the big firms operate? Does some kind of effective competition keep these corporations moving toward the best interests of society? Is there effective social control over these corporations and their economic behavior, or not? And what does the future hold in store on these questions? These are not easy questions to answer.

We really don't have an accepted theory of how a modern economic system works in the real world. We know that most prices are "administered" (that is, *set by somebody*) and we know that there is a lot of planning and long-range goal seeking, both by governments and by big businesses— much more than could exist in the neoclassical model of the market system. But how does it really work? We just don't have a generally accepted theory of that.

Those economists who hold strongest to the neoclassical tradition (the Chicago School) say that the real world still does approximate the neoclassical model. They say we shouldn't be looking for other ways of explaining the world. Some neoclassical economists have suggested that we should try to break up the big corporations—try to force real-world conditions to conform more closely to the assumed conditions of the neoclassical model.

Most economists don't think that the big modern corporations behave very much like the little typical firms described in the neoclassical model. Furthermore, most economists don't seem to think that the neoclassical prescription for solving the problem of bigness—by breaking up the big corporations—is very realistic or practical, either. So what explanation do most economists give? And what answer do they offer? That's the problem. Most of them don't have an explanation or an answer to offer. But one economist has: John Kenneth Galbraith. Let's take a look at what Galbraith has to say.

GALBRAITH'S CHALLENGE

It was in 1958 that Galbraith published *The Affluent Society,* attacking much of the "conventional wisdom" of modern-day economists. Nine years later (1967) he continued that attack in his book *The New Industrial State.* Then in 1973 he completed the attack and offered his solutions in *Economics and the Public Purpose.*

Galbraith raises serious questions about the applicability, the realism, and the helpfulness of the conventional wisdom in economics. He doesn't think the assumptions of the neoclassical model are close enough to reality. He thinks the results of the model are more misleading than helpful in understanding what really happens in the economies of the modern world. He thinks the neoclassical model and the things conventional economists do and say are more harmful than good, because the effect is to hide the truth about the things which are really *wrong* with the system. In the foreword of his latest book, *Economics and the Public Purpose,* he says: ". . . on no conclusion is this book more clear: Left to themselves, economic forces do not work out for the best except perhaps for the powerful."

Consumer Sovereignty and the Dependence Effect

Galbraith first attacks the idea of "consumer sovereignty"—the idea that the economic system is directed by and responds to the autonomous wishes of the people. He says that people's wants are not *independent* of the system, but are a *reflection* of the system. There is a kind of "keeping up with the Joneses" effect: as the economic system produces more things, new desires for those things are generated. So, says Galbraith, the system is responding to wants which it (the system) is *creating.* Galbraith calls this the "dependence effect."

If the dependence effect is granted, the idea of "consumer sovereignty" as the driving force in the economic system (as in the neoclassical model) doesn't make much sense anymore. No longer is the consumer rational in pursuing his objectives. As he spends he is responding to the influences of the system; he is not the ultimate source of power, the independent force, choosing the objectives to be sought and directing the economic system toward those objectives.

The Giant Corporation and the Technostructure

Galbraith's second major challenge to the neoclassical model is on the idea that businesses will adjust their behavior to try to get maximum profit. He focuses on the behavior of the giant corporations and points out that the big modern corporation is not run by a risk-taking entrepreneur. The guiding intelligence—the brain of the enterprise—is made up of many people with technical knowledge and talents who influence the group decisions which ultimately control the corporation. Galbraith calls this collective intelligence or "brain" of the organization the "technostructure"—not much like the risk-taking entrepreneur of the neoclassical model, right?

According to Galbraith, the technostructure wants to be a part of a *successful* organization. This means the corporation must *survive.* There must be adequate earnings. Also, it is important that the corporation grow. The first order of business of the technostructure is to avoid risks that might threaten the survival or growth of the company.

The technostructure would be in favor of government policies for stability of prices and employment; would not object to labor unions which would provide them a stable supply of labor and assure that labor costs would be more or less the same throughout the industrial system, eliminating the threat of competition from other producers with low-cost labor; would be in favor of high expenditures for education and skill development by the government, thus being assured an adequate supply of labor; and would be in favor of high government spending in technology-developing activities, such as in defense or the space program.

A Government-Industrial-Labor Complex?

Galbraith's view of the new industrial state is quite different from the dog-eat-dog world of maximum-profit-seeking competitive activity. He sees close parallels between the objectives of the industrial technostructure and those of many political leaders and labor leaders as well. All seek reasonable success in pursuing their objectives of stability and growth. He sees businesses and governments alike planning for long-range order and stability and movement toward predetermined objectives—a far cry from the automatic operation of the laissez-faire market system described by Adam Smith and the neoclassical economists!

Galbraith doesn't see a total elimination of competition, but he sees competition more between *industries* than between firms in the same industry. The steel industry must be careful lest it lose more and more of its markets to aluminum, plastics, and other metals and metal substitutes. This is the only kind of competition that effectively operates between the massive corporations in Galbraith's "new industrial state."

Galbraith sees a tendency to overemphasize *economic* goals. The technostructure wants to increase production, incomes, employment, consumption, and all that. There is no place in the corporate planning process for placing proper emphasis on the noneconomic objectives and goals which the society might wish to pursue—goals which may be more important in an affluent society than the "economic" or "material" objectives and goals! So what does Galbraith prescribe? Let's talk about that.

The Galbraithian Prescription: The New Socialisms

In his former books, Galbraith diagnoses the problems. In *Economics and the Public Purpose,* he prescribes. What does he prescribe? A vastly different kind of economic system than the one which exists (or which most economists seem to *think* exists) in the United States today. He suggests:

Government takeover and operation of the sectors of the economy which have not been adequately serving the needs of the society, such as housing, urban transportation, and medical care;

Government actions to strengthen the small businesses which still operate as a market sector in the economy, but which are at a disadvantage against the giant corporations;

Government guaranteed annual income;

Government planning, coordination, and controls over the big corporations (including controls over wages and prices in the big corporations); and

Government nationalization of the big defense contractors.

Essentially, Galbraith wants (a) the industries which can't perform adequately to be run by the government; (b) the big corporations and technostructure planning to be brought under government planning; (c) the remainder of the economy to be strengthened so that it can operate effectively as a *free market* sector, and (d) more income redistribution by government to reduce "unearned" incomes and to more nearly eliminate poverty.

What about these Galbraithian ideas? Are they feasible? Or too radical to contemplate? Galbraith says, "practical necessity has already forced a measure of practical action" along the lines suggested. He says that what he is really doing is providing "the theoretical justification for what circumstances and good sense have already initiated."

Here again, as with John Maynard Keynes, Adam Smith, and others, we find an economist looking at the undeniable problems in the world—watching what's wrong, seeing what's being done—and then offering an explanation. Galbraith offers mankind a new way of looking at and approaching the economic issues and problems of the last quarter of the twentieth century. But, fortunately or unfortunately, the image of the world which Galbraith describes is not the image which most economists or most people in the United States are ready to accept. Therefore the Galbraithian prescription is not likely to be taken very soon—certainly not in very large doses.

Galbraith, Keynes, Veblen—Challengers to Conventional Wisdom

Galbraith, like Keynes and like Veblen before him, has walked (and today continues to walk) a path quite distinctly different from that of the conventional economist of the day. All three of these men have broken step with the profession in order to turn their attention more directly to the problems and issues of the day. In so doing, all three have lost many friends and gained some (perhaps bitter) enemies.

I suppose that anyone who breaks ranks with his colleagues and then mounts an effective attack on their hallowed beliefs is bound to be criticized. Galbraith (like Keynes and Veblen) has many critics. But judging from what one can find out, neither Galbraith nor Keynes nor Veblen was bothered in the least by the flurries of criticism which their pioneering ideas generated. Likely, only people strong enough to withstand a withering fire of criticism could ever perform the pioneering function of a Veblen, a Keynes, or a Galbraith.

The Effects of the Giant Corporations?
We Don't Know

So what can we say about the present and future effects of giant corporations in the U. S. and world economies? And about Galbraith's new way of looking at and explaining the way a modern industrial economy functions? And about his recommended "New Socialisms" for changing the economic system to better serve the society? I'm sorry, but we really don't know. It's just too complex an issue. Things are changing *so fast,* it's just too early to tell.

Anyone in touch with the modern industrial society knows there's truth in what Galbraith says. But how much? And what does this tell us about the "social efficiency" of the modern industrial market-oriented economic society? And should we embark on a program aimed toward the Galbraithian prescription? In the coming years, economists, business and political leaders, policy makers, and others will be digging into these issues—trying to figure them out better. If you'd like to become an economist and help us, *welcome!* We need all the help we can get. But now, time for a new problem—the environmental problem.

THE CRISIS OF THE ENVIRONMENT

While the very efficient and highly motivating market system was supporting industrial growth by leaps and bounds, society was coming closer and closer to solving its traditional economic problem—how to provide food and other material necessities to the people. But at the same time the market system was setting the stage for the creation of a new and serious problem—the problem of the ecological balance between an industrial society and its environment.

As the Industrial Revolution broke loose, outputs expanded. Then population began expanding more and more. As the decades passed, both these influences—increasing outputs and increasing numbers of people—began to build up an environmental problem. Now that problem is acute.

The Automatic Market Mechanism Doesn't Protect the Environment

How did it happen that the market system, which is supposed to direct the society's resources into *desirable* channels, allowed the environmental problem to arise? Why didn't the market system protect society against it? The answer is simple: The environmental problem is outside the market, just as the population expansion problem is. There is no way that the automatic market process can handle these problems.

These *many* decades since the Industrial Revolution, we have been living high without paying the full costs of what we have been getting from the earth. We have been pulling natural resources from the earth without having to incur the costs of reproducing or recycling those natural resources. We have been dumping wastes into the environment without having to pay the costs of cleaning up the wastes. But now we are in a situation where something must be done.

Too many resources are being pulled out of the environment and too many wastes are being put back into the environment. It is already going too fast to be sustained. To dramatize the problem some people refer to our planet as "spaceship earth." We're flying through space on a finite world; when we use up all of our supplies, then we will all die. Like it or not, that's just the way it is. Economist Kenneth Boulding is one who emphasizes this problem. Boulding says that we must begin to think of recycling *everything*, and replacing *everything* which we take from nature. We must dump *nothing* into the environment which natural forces cannot handle—that is, which nature cannot recycle.

The Human Herd Is Getting Too Big for the Range

What about the *population* aspect of the problem of ecological imbalance? At the beginning of this century there were only about 1.5 billion people on earth. Today there are about four billion. At current rates of growth, by the middle of the next century there will be about sixteen billion.

But there's just no way so many people can be supported on the earth! Not unless we find a lot of unbelievable ways to recycle things, and to generate something out of nothing.

What's going to happen? Two things will happen, because they *must* happen. (1) Somehow the population expansion will be slowed, and (ultimately) stopped. (2) *All* productive activities will begin shifting more and more energy toward recycling materials and toward protecting and rebuilding the natural environment. The normal processes of life in all the advanced nations must go through some changes. There's no doubt about it.

The High "Real Cost" of Protecting the Environment

The recycling and environmental protection efforts are going to cost a lot. Many resources, much energy, much valuable effort will be required. *All* products are likely to cost a lot more before very long.

Maybe the people of the United States and the other advanced nations are about to see an actual *decline* in their level of material welfare. If a lot of resources, energy, capital, and labor are diverted toward environmental rebuilding, recycling, and pollution control, that will mean a lot more energy and resources used up as *costs of production.* So we will get a lot less output for our used up inputs. That will mean fewer goods for the people.

Will our standards of living actually go *down*? No one knows, of course. But it's quite possible. The inputs used for environmental protection (like the gallon of gas your car burns to run the antipollution equipment) must come from somewhere. Those inputs sure can't be used to do or make what they were doing or making before. The energy (gas) your car uses up for pollution control can't also be used to make your car go.

Both the population problem and the environmental problem must be solved. No question about it. But how? Must the government get involved? You know the answer. *Of course* the government must get involved. The government must get involved on the population and environmental issues, on the giant corporations and monopoly power issues, on the unemployment and inflation issues, and on many other important issues which haven't even been talked about in this book. Why must the government get involved? Because there's just no other way. People demand that these problems be attacked. Government provides the only realistic avenue of attack. Is it any wonder that in all the market-oriented societies of the world today, the role of the state in economic affairs is increasing? That governments are getting involved, more and more? When you think about it, it makes sense. Why? Because there's no choice. If we're going to do anything to try to solve the problems, there's just no other way.

It's time to talk about that now—about increasing government involvement in the economic choices of modern society—about a trend to which there seems to be no realistic alternative—about how real-world economic systems are changing—about the increasing role of the state in the economic systems of the free nations of the modern world—about "the socialization of capitalism."

THE CONTINUING EVOLUTION OF THE
WORLD'S ECONOMIC SYSTEMS

Throughout history economic systems have been changing. But it wasn't until recent centuries that the changes began to become big, and cumulative—like a chain reaction, like a row of tumbling dominos. One thing leads to another and onward and upward we go!

Feudal society eroded, people were shaken loose from their land and from their traditional roles in life; trade expanded and the *market system* evolved. Remember? Then the Industrial Revolution added much more speed to the progressive changes, and the modern economic systems evolved out of all that.

The Market Process Can't Solve All the Problems

Then the tough problems of this century began to batter society from several sides—wars, inflation, depression, economic power of giant businesses, population explosion, poverty, pollution, the urban crisis, and others. What about all these problems? They all require that some of society's resources be directed toward solutions. Yet how can that happen? The *market system* doesn't automatically direct resources toward wars and environmental protection and inflation and depression and all. So how can the problems be handled? The government must do it.

The government must play a more important role in the resource-directing process. More of the society's choices must be made by the government—through the political processes of the society. That is to say: The economic system must change to include fewer market-directed choices and more government-directed choices. Is that what's going on in the world? Yes, that's exactly what's happening.

The Increasing Role of the State

In all free economies of the modern world, the role of the government (the state) has been increasing in recent years. Urgent problems of modern society have required it. This trend is still going on, and it will continue. Why? Because the market system operating by itself can't deal with the problems that must be dealt with, that's why!

The governments must get increasingly involved in planning—in setting goals and in directing various activities in the economy. As this happens, the free market economic systems evolve into something else—something different from either the model or the reality of traditional capitalism.

How far will the market systems change in response to the needs of modern society? No one knows, really. I suppose it's safe to say that it will go as far and as fast as practical necessity and political expediency take it. It's an interesting and suspenseful drama to watch. It makes some people sad, some bewildered. But that's always the way with rapid change.

As the modern economic systems change, what about capitalism? Will capitalism survive? Just for a minute, let's talk about that.

What About the Survival of Capitalism?

Questions about the survival of capitalism really don't make much sense. What is capitalism? Capitalism *was* the economic system of the mid-nineteenth century, observed and attacked (and incidentally, named) by Karl Marx. That kind of economic system doesn't exist anywhere in the world. It hasn't for more than forty years! To talk about the survival of the system Marx called capitalism would be an irrelevant, purely academic exercise.

The names we use for economic systems these days really don't offer very accurate descriptions of anything. Capitalism, socialism, and communism have become words to argue about. The words don't describe any real-world economic systems. These words—creations of nineteenth-century social protest philosopher–prophets—have become the banners in a kind of worldly religious struggle. The whole argument is far more emotional than rational, and far more political than economic. We would all understand economic systems a lot better, and likely the twentieth-century world would be a much more pleasant place to live, if everyone would forget about these worldly religions. Better we should confine our discussions to the *substance* of different economic systems and forget about the emotion-packed names by which they are known.

We've Solved the Old Problems and Created New Ones

The problems of modern civilization are pressing more and more on all people, everywhere. These problems have been visited upon us by our own progress. We have gone so far toward solving the old problems—hunger, disease, others—that we have uncovered (or permitted to arise) new problems.

The new problems have been allowed to arise only because they have not been held in check by the powerful automatic social control mechanism which brought the great progress. What mechanism? The *market process,* of course! So now how does society take charge and take action on these new kinds of problems? By building new kinds of control mechanisms, of course—mechanisms which will be effective over things which the *market process* cannot effectively control. Obvious once you think about it, isn't it?

HAS THE MARKET SYSTEM HAD ITS DAY IN THE SUN?

What powered the great thrust of economic growth which tore the world loose from its traditional past and brought us to this seething modern world of violent change? The market system? Right!

The Market Process Generated the Modern World

The high-living, bewildering modern world was generated by the powerful motivating and controlling forces of the market process:

> the harsh law-of-the-jungle system of rewards and punishments, where the productive people are rewarded and the others go hungry;
>
> the powerful incentive of *profits,* stimulating more production and greater efficiency; and
>
> the powerful force of prices, conserving and rationing the society's resources, and motivating the production of more of the wanted things.

These powerful forces of the market process were responsible for the economic breakthroughs which generated the modern world.

People, businesses, nations, all were striving, conserving, pushing to get ahead. They wanted the pleasure of having lots of things. Everyone wanted to try to get ahead of everyone else. People were highly motivated, working, producing. As the market system stimulated the production of the things people and businesses were buying, more and better goods became available. New kinds of goods became available— consumer goods; capital goods. More and better machines, equipment, factories—things needed to increase productivity even more.

The market process provided a way to channel *self interest*—to use this powerful force as the *energy* to thrust the economy forward, to speed up production and generate rapid economic growth. We who live in the advanced nations would be able to have only a fraction of the things we now enjoy, were it not for the powerful motivating and controlling forces of the market process. So what now? Is that all over and done with? And if so, why? What happens next?

The Pure Market System Is No Longer Socially Acceptable

Throughout the world the modern market-oriented economies are more and more turning away from the market process. The political process—government direction and control—is making and carrying out more and more of society's economic choices. Governments everywhere are bypassing or overthrowing the directives of the market process. It's happening in the advanced nations and in the less-developed countries, too. The less-developed countries are devising government plans and using administrative directions and controls to try to steer their economies toward their longed-for goals of economic development. Why is the powerful market process being ignored and abandoned? There are several reasons.

Many things about the way the market process works are not so acceptable anymore (some never were, really). Inequality is one problem—great wealth, with things being used lavishly and wasted by the rich while the poor go hungry.

All modern market-oriented nations have developed programs to lessen the inequality generated by the market system. The modern nations produce enough so that even the poor can be adequately provided for, so governments are overthrowing the "distribution choice" of the market process and shifting more of the output to the poor.

Another problem, to some people, is the emphasis on selfishness as the *motive force* which makes the market process work. Some people don't like the idea of giving rewards to those who do selfish things. Selfishness has proven to be a very powerful and highly efficient force for driving the economic system (and also for achieving the survival of most living things). But most people don't consider selfishness to be much of a human virtue.

But there is an even more basic problem than inequality or the emphasis on selfishness. An inherent flaw, perhaps? An inability of the freely operating market process to protect and work for society's best interest? So it seems. Sometimes it is impossible for the freely operating market process to reflect and respond to the true wishes of the society. *That's* the problem.

The market process directs the society's resources to "flow toward the dollar"—that is, to go where, and to do what the *spenders* wish. The uses of all of the society's things are determined by the ways in which the people spend their money. So what's the problem? Just that in the modern world, that arrangement can't always optimize the use of society's resources in working toward the true objectives and goals of the society. This is an important issue; we need to go into it a little deeper.

*The Free Market Process Cannot Set Goals
for Society*

There are many ways in which a modern society's true objectives are not reflected in the market process. Many desired objectives cannot be achieved simply by letting resources be directed into whatever the people spend their money for—and into nothing else. This arrangement would leave many important functions inadequately performed—perhaps not performed at all. What functions? The traditional ones are such things as education, fire and police protection, roads and streets, public welfare, national defense, health and hospitals, perhaps urban housing, perhaps others.

Most people have agreed for a long time that the *political process* must direct some resources into these "public" functions—that the market process acting alone can't look out for the society's best interests in these areas. But now, suddenly (almost overnight!), this *kind* of problem is exploding all over the landscape! So many cases where the free market process can't look out for the society's best interests anymore.

What's the problem? Economists call it "externalities." It's the "spill-over effect" that happens almost every time anybody does *anything* these days.

The Problem of Externalities—the "Spill-Over Effect"

The free market process just can't control the spill-over effects—the things that happen outside the market—things like air and water pollution that don't influence the *costs* and *prices* of things. The market process would force the producer to use cheap fuel, dirty the air, and sell his product at a low price. But the *true* social objectives would require more expensive fuel, cleaner air, and a higher-priced product.

Before there were such great increases in population and industrialization, there wasn't much of a problem of externalities. But now all modern societies face the *urgent* and *unavoidable* task of bringing our heavily populated, heavily industrialized modern world into ecological balance with our natural environment. And how can the free market process do that? That's the problem. It can't.

So what must happen? The society must go after these problems some other way? Of course. And what other way is there? The political process? Government plans, regulations, controls, charges, penalties, subsidies, and such? Of course. That's the only way.

So many social choices can no longer be decided on the basis of how the people choose to spend their money. The free market process cannot direct all the choices in the society's best interests, so the political process must get involved. Governments must overthrow some of the choice-making power of the market process, must define the essential objectives, and must arrange for energy and other resources to be used to achieve the chosen objectives. Governments *must* do it. There's just no other way.

So has the market process had its day in the sun? Has it "done its thing" in ripping out the social control mechanisms that kept societies stable (and alive) for thousands of years? In its brief moment on stage it has blasted mankind off on this bewildering journey. Many people now realize that we must alter the course of our journey. Quickly. So, must we push the free market process off stage after such a short (but brilliant!) performance? Not entirely. But to a considerable extent, yes. Or at least so it seems.

The Market Process: From Master to Servant of Social Choice

Throughout the last century and up to the depression of the 1930s the forces of the free market process really were in charge. The market process really was acting as "master control" over the society's resources. Private individuals and businesses, responding to market forces, determined for the economy *what* was going to happen and *where, when, how,* and *how much.* The free forces of the market process really did provide the avenue of social choice. But since World War I (in Europe) and especially since the depression of the 1930s (in the U. S.), the choice-making power of the free market process has more and more been modified, restrained, and pushed aside.

It isn't that markets and market forces have been abolished. Incentives and rewards still operate. Prices are still conserving things and motivating the production of things. The drive to get ahead and the attractiveness of profits still motivate people. So what's happening? What is the nature of this change that's occurring?

It is partly a tempering of the market forces themselves. Taxes on wages and profits change the "incentive force" somewhat; welfare payments and payments to unemployed people reduce somewhat the discomfort of being unproductive. And there are other ways the market forces have been lessened. But that isn't the really big issue. Much more important—especially for the continuing long-run evolution of the world's economic systems—is this:

> The market process for a fleeting moment in history was the powerful, disruptive *master* of social choice. Now it is being broken to harness—forced into the role of *servant* to carry out the deliberate (we hope, *rational*) resource-use choices of the society—choices made by (and in view of objectives and goals chosen by) the local, state, and national governments—that is, by the political processes of the society.

How is it possible for the role of the market process to be changed from master to servant? After you read the next two subsections you will understand.

Society's Economic Problem: The Production and Distribution Questions

Each society faces its economic problem—of dealing with scarcity, of deciding what to do with each of its scarce resources: What to use and what to save. What to do and what to make. Who will get to have how much of what. Those are the choices which, somehow, the society must make. That's the society's economic problem.

Usually economists break down the economic problem into (1) the *production* question (deciding what things to produce, in what quantities, using how much of which inputs and what production techniques, and so on), and (2) the *distribution* question (deciding how big a share of the output each person will get).

How does a society get the answers to these questions? Through its economic system, of course. That's the purpose of the economic system—to work out the answers to these questions. Each economic system uses some combination of (1) the social process (following the traditional ways of answering the questions), (2) the political process (government decisions), and (3) the market process (letting resources flow to meet the demands of the people). These breakdowns:

> of the *economic problem* into "production" and "distribution" questions, and

> of the *economic-problem-solving techniques* into "social," "political," and "market" processes,

are helpful. But there's another way these questions can be broken down.

To understand what's happening right now in the rapid evolution of the world's economic systems—for example, to understand the shifting role of the market process from master to servant of social choice—we need a new breakdown. We need a breakdown between (1) economic *decision-making* (*choosing* the objectives and goals), and (2) the *implementation* of economic decisions (*directing resources* to achieve the chosen objectives and goals).

Society's Economic Problem: The Decision-Making and Implementation Questions

Solving a society's economic problem involves not one but *two* functions: (1) *making* the choices, and (2) *carrying out* the choices. Why is it so important to separate these two functions? Just this: One process (for example, the political process) may be used to *make* the decision, while another process (for example, the market process) may be used to *carry out* the decision. And that's important.

Now do you begin to see what has been happening to the role of the market process? Of course! Its *decision-making* function more and more is being stripped away; its *implementation* function is being used more and more to carry out *political process decisions*! Is that how the market process has been shifting from the role of *master* of social choice, to the role of *servant*? Of course. Servant to the society's will, as expressed by the society's political processes.

Just as the market process can both *make* and *carry out* the economic choices for society, so can the political process perform both functions. The Soviet Union, the People's Republic of China ("Red China"), and other Communist (that is, neo-Marxian socialist) countries rely almost entirely on their political processes to perform both functions—to make and to carry out the choices. Generally the plans are implemented by administrators who direct resources into the necessary uses to carry out the government's plans.

However, in recent years the Communist countries have been discovering the efficiency of the market process as servant to the political process. They are finding out how easy it is to get labor and other resources to move in the desired directions by offering wage and price incentives. The market-oriented countries at the same time are becoming more aware of the real-world limitations on the ability of the market process, acting alone, to protect the society's resources and to generate optimal levels of social well-being. So they are shifting more of the *decision-making* function to the political process.

The Converging Evolution of the World's Economic Systems

So what's happening? The Communist countries are slowly changing their economic systems to take more advantage of the highly efficient market process as an *implementation* device. At the same time, the market-oriented countries are introducing more and more government planning, stripping the market process of its decision-making role, but usually depending on the market process to carry out the plans.

As the economic systems of the world evolve it seems inevitable that more of the choices in the market-oriented economies will be made through the political process. But it's likely that the market process will continue to be used to implement the plans. Why? Because the market process is highly efficient. No resource administrator needs to work out each little detail. People and resources move automatically in response to the market-process incentives. And with the market process, people have more freedom of choice. No one needs to be ordered around. Price adjustments can be used to pull more (or fewer) resources in each direction.

While the market-oriented societies are learning more about how to use the political process in setting goals and objectives and designing plans, the Communist countries are learning more about how to use the market process to increase their efficiency in implementing their plans. In most of the less-developed countries too, political-process planning with market-process implementation seems to offer the most effective approach for achieving the desired development objectives.

So is everyone happy with these changes in their economic systems? No—far from it. Many people in the United States and other market-oriented countries take capitalism as a sort of religion and argue against any government goal-setting and planning. (Government planning is communistic!) Many people in the Soviet Union and other neo-Marxian socialist countries take communism as a sort of religion and argue against any use of the market process to implement their plans. (Price and profit incentives are capitalistic!) But as times are changing, people are changing their minds. Perhaps someday these narrow attitudes will pass into history. If so, the world is likely to get along a lot better after that.

There's another kind of problem, too. First, it isn't easy for socio-economic planners to figure out exactly how to harness the market process so the economy is directed toward the desired objectives. It takes a lot of expert economic understanding and analysis to figure out what ought to be done. Second, even if the planners knew exactly what to do, the political realities of *politics* often would prevent them from carrying out their well-designed plans. Still, somehow it's being done—not always done *well,* but being done, because it must be done. There's more and more planning in the "free" economies, and more and more use of the market process in the "planned" economies.

So what happens now? What does the future hold in store? Will all of the economic systems of the world soon look pretty much alike? Of course not! But it does seem that as the years go by the world's economic systems will come to look *more* alike. You can see why. Maybe as the evolution proceeds, mankind will discover even better ways to organize and run its economic systems. Let's hope so.

NEEDED: NEW WORLDWIDE SOCIAL CONTROL MECHANISMS

Back in ancient times and feudal times—and in some societies even today—a structure of "nonmarket-type" social control mechanisms held the society together, prevented things which would have been socially destructive, and made possible the *survival* of the society. But then came the erosion of the traditional societies and the emergence and growth of the powerful market process, pushing all else aside and thrusting forward the explosive development of modern society.

What now? Are we about to go full circle? Throughout most of the time man has been on earth, the traditional social control mechanisms of the clan, the tribe, the manor, and other such social organizations have "kept it all together." Must *world society* now begin to develop social control mechanisms to try to achieve for all of us what the traditional social control mechanisms achieved for the traditional societies? Has the powerful market process, as *master of social choice,* had its day in the sun—now to be relegated to the role of *servant* to the socio-economic planners? And if so, how do we expect these national and worldwide changes in economic systems to come about?

These are interesting and critical questions—worthy of the most serious thoughts of the very best minds the world can produce. It's really important that we come up with the right answers. Mankind's survival might depend on it.

EPILOG
THE ECONOMICS OF YESTERDAY,
TODAY, AND TOMORROW — AN OVERVIEW

Think for a moment about the broad sweep of history you've been reading about in this book: first the thousands of centuries man has been on earth; then, about 3000 BC, the cradles of civilization. Twenty-five more centuries went by, then came the city-states of ancient Greece and Rome. Another five centuries passed before the Roman Empire began (at about the time of Christ). After five centuries of the Roman Empire, about AD 500, the medieval period began. Ten more centuries passed before the discovery of America and the development of mercantilism; another three centuries before the American colonies became a nation and the Industrial Revolution got underway.

Throughout all these hundreds of centuries, throughout recorded history and before, surely you would think there *must* have been *some* people who were observing the miseries of mankind, trying to change and improve things, trying to suggest better ways. Observing, yes. Explaining, yes. But trying to change things? Generally, no. The societies were controlled by tradition, remember? The customs and taboos of the society told people what their "lot" was—what they were supposed to do and how life was supposed to be. Mostly, people just accepted things as they were.

Until Recently, Stable, Traditional Society Has Been the Norm

Every person sort of played the same role as his parents and grandparents, facing the same problems that people had always faced. There was no disruptive social upheaval except when some conquering ruler's armies came in and changed things. Some few philosophers wrote about economic matters, about "the material conditions of mankind," and about what was good and what was bad in matters of exchange, production, and all that. But in general the philosophies and ideas expressed were aimed toward *maintaining the stability* of society—*preventing change.*

Remember the implicit objective of *social stability* reflected in the writings of Aristotle? And then later in the writings of the Christian philosophers of the medieval period? It was not until the Industrial Revolution came along to sort of "blow up" the traditional social structures that big changes began to occur. And it wasn't until then that the philosophers began to play in a much larger ball park—no longer restricted by the necessity to place high value on the traditional concept of social stability; liberated from the bonds of traditional ideas of monarchy, nobility, class structure, and from the traditional concepts of "right" and "wrong" in production, exchange, and prices. They were free to raise some serious questions about what was happening, and about what ought to be happening.

Breaking Loose From the Bonds of Tradition

Suddenly this new "liberalism" erupted in the writings of Adam Smith and Thomas Jefferson and Jeremy Bentham and others. Suddenly many traditionally accepted beliefs were coming under attack. As the world was undergoing the violent change of the Industrial Revolution, economic-social-political thinking was responding—was going through its own violent change, touched off by what was happening in the world.

The new ball game begun by the industrial revolution—the population expansions and migrations and the breaking loose of just about everything—began only about two hundred years ago, but it amounted to the greatest change mankind has ever seen in all of his thousands of centuries on earth. Only recently has mankind pushed aside his "normal" relationship with nature and gained tremendous power to adapt and change and control nature. With this power man has become capable of supporting greatly increased numbers of people on earth.

Explosive Change Destroyed the "Natural Balance"

But the explosive change in the condition of mankind, and in the relationships between mankind and earth, has upset things. All kinds of disruptive influences and chain reactions have gotten underway. But there have been no parallel developments for maintaining harmony among people, or between mankind and the environment. Now suddenly it's beginning to appear that the ultimate survival of mankind may depend on the speedy development of some new kinds of social-control mechanisms—mechanisms which will pull things back into balance—maintain harmony among people and among nations, and between people and the environment.

What created the problem? The violently disruptive influences of (1) the Industrial Revolution, and (2) the free market system. Working together these two forces generated great savings and massive investments in new and better capital—factories, machines, equipment, mass production. Productivity increased rapidly. Each increase in capital brought more productivity; each increase in productivity brought more profit, more savings, more investment, more capital, and even *more* productivity. The rate of economic growth was unbelievable—far surpassing anything the world had ever seen or anyone had ever before *conceived.* The farther it went, the faster it got—rapid growth, feeding on itself, fueling the fires of its own rocket engines.

Economic Growth Becomes Explosive

Any kind of cumulative, progressive change which feeds on itself, fueling the fires of its own engines, speeding faster and faster, ultimately becomes *explosive.* Sooner or later it's bound to run into some problems. Right? Of course. That's what has happened. And here we are caught in the midst of it all, not knowing quite what's going on or what to do—and aware that if we *did* know what ought to be done, probably no one would listen, anyway.

Does the growth process now need to be stopped? Or slowed? Some say yes; some say no. We really don't know. By the time we know the answer, likely it will be too late for the answer to do us much good, anyway. Hindsight, not foresight, will let all of us see it. Meanwhile, questions about the long-range economic-social-political impact of the economic growth rate of the world aren't likely to be uppermost in the minds of most people.

Agenda for the '70s: Brushfire Problems and Symptom-Treating

It's likely that over the next few decades the immediate, pressing, "brushfire" problems will be taking most of the attention: inflation, unemployment, monopoly, acute environmental problems, shortages of some resources, poverty, the urban crisis, and other acute problems. On the inflation–unemployment issue, probably some kind of "neo-Keynesian, monetarist, wage-price guidelines" synthesis will somehow emerge, will restore the confidence of the business and financial community in the government's ability to regulate the economy, and will work. I hope so.

It's likely that pragmatic "symptom-treating" (rub on the salve wherever it hurts) will be used to deal with most of modern society's emerging problems—monopoly, environmental destruction, poverty, urban blight, resource shortages, and others. As each problem becomes too acute to be tolerated, some direct symptom-treating action will be taken. If the first dose doesn't ease the pain, something more or different will be done. That's the way things have been going; that's the way things seem likely to keep going.

The Theorist-Explainers and the Activist-Changers

Think back over the past two-hundred years of explosive change. Think of the people—the philosophers and protestors and activists you have been reading about. I suppose we could think of these people as falling into two groups: those who were most concerned with trying to *understand* and *explain* what was happening, and those who were most concerned with trying to *change* things. The classical and neoclassical economists were the "theorist-explainers;" the utopian socialists and communist revolutionaries were the "activist-changers."

There were a few, like Marx, who managed to play both games. But not many. Generally, those who were trying to *explain* things thought those who were trying to change things were wasting their time. The natural economic forces would trip them up at every turn; their attempts to change things would only make matters worse. But those who were trying to *change* things, the activist-changers, condemned the theorist-explainers as being unproductive and irrelevant—unwilling to get involved in direct social action to try to improve things.

Is the situation much different, today? No, not really. We still have the theorists trying to explain things and the activists working for change. Each blames the other for indulging in irrelevant or unproductive or ill-conceived and misdirected pursuits. The theorists accuse the activists of doing naive things—things which could never work within the real-world laws of economics. The activists accuse the theorists of being irrelevant, out of touch with the real problems of the world, playing little games in their ivory towers.

The world has changed drastically over the last two centuries, but the people haven't changed all that much. Perhaps it's good that each generation seems to produce some theorists and some activists. Perhaps each group helps to keep the other on its toes.

Almost Everything Has Changed, Just Since You Were Born!

Now just look at all the changes that have been happening in your lifetime—changes in production methods, outputs, real income; changes in attitudes toward poverty, education, nationalism, wage rates, profits, war; toward the issues of urbanization, pollution, land uses; toward the economic, social, and political rights of racial minorities, of women, of young people; and all the new technology—computers, transistors, solid state electronics, polio prevention, space travel; attitudes toward dress, personal appearance, family relationships, student-professor relationships, work and leisure, wealth, home ownership, alcohol, marijuana, marriage, sex, criminal punishment; the role of government—you name it. Generation gap? Confusion? Frustration? Bewilderment? My God! How could it be otherwise?

People who are still thinking by the standards and conditions of the 1930s, the '40s, the '50s,—the '60s, even!—are already far behind the times—out of touch. No wonder it's tough to reach agreement on anything anymore! No wonder it's a real struggle to get a "representative" candidate for the U. S. presidency. No wonder it's tough on students who have to go through school and college under the surveillance and tutelage of so many different people—many people whose minds (unfortunately) were "programmed and locked in" during various different time periods in the past.

How Do We Learn to Cope with Change?

It's just sort of miraculous that any of you who are students today manage to make it without having your personalities completely destroyed! But maybe, after all, this is the best way for education to help you to learn to adapt, to cope in a world of explosive change. Maybe this is the best way to ensure that your mind will learn to keep growing to meet the new challenges which are destined to confront you almost daily throughout your lifetime. Perhaps the frustrating college experience you're going through will help to ensure that throughout your life you won't be left back here in "the dark ages" of the 1970s.

The world today has plenty of brilliant and well-educated people whose ideas are mostly irrelevant simply because they haven't developed the built-in mental flexibility and adaptability needed to enable them to catch up and keep up with this explosively changing world. They're just sort of left in the wake as time speeds on by.

There will always be many people who can't (or who don't want to) keep up. Maybe that's good—a stabilizing influence perhaps. But such people will always be a little bewildered. And they will be very frustrated each time their lives are touched by each new manifestation of "the new tomorrow"—like when the government decides to raise taxes, or subsidize medical care, or to nationalize the railroads—or when junior decides to let his hair grow or daughter decides to move into the coed dorm.

Society Is Doing the Split Between Past and Future—Which Foot Do You Want to Be?

Perhaps it's good that society in each decade has one foot firmly planted on the known ground of the past while the other foot moves, seeking to find some better place to stand on the uncertain ground of the future. It's up to each of us—you, me, everyone—to decide, on each issue: Which role do I want to play? Which foot do I want to be?

There's no easy way to decide. No easy answer. Maybe the historical perspective you've gained from this little book will sometimes help you to make the right decision. I hope so.

INDEX